# Diagramming the Scriptures

## Systematic Approach to Sentence Diagramming

### Textbook

Shirley M. Forsen

Copyright © 2010 by Shirley M. Forsen

*Diagramming the Scriptures*
by Shirley M. Forsen

Printed in the United States of America

ISBN 9781609572655

All rights reserved solely by the author. The author guarantees all contents are original and do not infringe upon the legal rights of any other person or work. No part of this book may be reproduced in any form without the permission of the author. The views expressed in this book are not necessarily those of the publisher.

Unless otherwise indicated, Bible quotations are taken from the King James Version. Copyright © 2000 by Holman Bible Publishers.

www.xulonpress.com

## Acknowledgements

The Lord Jesus Christ provided the guidance, strength, and perseverance. To Him goes all the glory and praise!

To my brother and his wife, George and Margaret Forsen, and my sister, Dixie Kidney, I owe deep gratitude for all their financial and prayerful support and encouragement.

Many friends have prayed for me for years; I could not have finished the book without their steadfast praying.

Dr. Jim Anderson, chancellor of Midwestern Baptist College, approved the choices of sections of the Scripture verses used.

Helen Budinger, Tricia Collier, and Becky Klein were vital sources of computer expertise and assistance.

Indispensable help came from residents of Foxwood Springs: Betty Goode, Darrell Hampton, Lee Keith, Kenneth Scott, Rowena Shaffer, Marjorie Slavens, and Art Tees.

Becky Young contributed to the instructions for the teacher and the student.

Laura and Stephen Blunk, homeschoolers, made great suggestions for improving the book and presented the book with me to the residents of Foxwood Springs Living Center.

The editor for the book was David Schneeberger. Proofreaders were Diana Anderson, Cathy Beard, Nancy Dillon, Glada Kelley, Helen Nichols, Lynn Pohle, and Nancy Ratcliffe.

# Preface

*Diagramming the Scriptures* serves two purposes: to teach sentence diagramming and to teach the Scriptures. *Every* word in a sentence (verse) has a certain place in a diagram. This blueprint helps a person to "see" or understand what has been written. The end product is a solid foundation of the English language.

The value of knowing the Bible is inestimable. Without knowledge of the Bible, understanding of much literature, music, law, history, and government is limited. William McKinley, the twenty-fifth President of the United States (1843-1901), said, "The more profoundly we study this wonderful book (the Bible), and the more closely we observe its divine precepts, the better citizens we will become and the higher will be our destiny as a nation." Jesus himself quoted from Deuteronomy: "But he (Jesus) answered and said, 'It is written, "Man shall not live by bread alone, but by every word that proceedeth out of the mouth of God"'" (Matthew 4:4).

My prayer is that this book will help the student to break the Bread into edible bites for easier digestion and to lay a firm foundation for speaking and writing of the English language.

# Instructions to the Teacher

Diagramming allows practice and application for grammar rules previously introduced and learned. This workbook could be used as a supplement to grammar instruction.

## Master Teacher Plan

For each lesson the teacher will do the following:

1. Introduce form.
2. Define new terms.
3. Show and explain examples.
4. Guide student practice - Practice Sheet(s).
5. Review.
6. Assess student progress mastery - Test Sheet.

For each unit the teacher will do the following:

1. Review the unit(s).
2. Assess student progress mastery - Unit Test.

For all four units the teacher will do the following:

1. Review the units.
2. Assess student progress mastery - Final Test.

## Lesson Plan Notes for the Teacher

First, the student should memorize and master the five sentence patterns.

Next, the student will begin the diagramming lessons. Some lesson plans will have necessary words defined. All lessons have examples, a place for practice, and an assessment of mastery.

The first diagramming formula divides a simple sentence between the subject and the predicate.

The first five sentences are diagrammed to demonstrate this beginning formula. Review each example with students. Read aloud the first sentence. Diagram the sentence on the board or on a transparency. Explain why the entire sentence is underlined, and point out why there is a vertical line between the subject and the predicate.

For this first day of diagramming, move slowly! Students must understand that the purpose of diagramming is to enhance their understanding of how grammar works. Diagramming is merely a picture of the pieces and parts of grammar. It is a graphic organizer.

After introduction and explanation of the first five sentences and diagrams, student will practice diagramming the next five sentences. Use the blank diagram models for this practice.

## Lesson Plan Notes for the Teacher

Check students' work for accuracy and understanding. If there are frequent mistakes, review the first examples.

Next, instruct students to read the last set of sentences. The students will copy one sentence at a time and diagram each new sentence. Check frequently for understanding.

A test after each section of diagrams will reinforce what the student has learned in the previous lesson(s).

Last, there is a final assessment of student mastery. This test covers all the sentence patterns, parts of speech, clauses, and sentence types that have been diagrammed in the book.

# Instructions to Student

Diagramming is a series of formulas. Once you have mastered the formulas, you will understand and apply the grammar rules you have learned. Writing won't be a dreaded task.

First, you will learn the five basic sentence patterns (formulas) for the English language. You will learn many new terms as you study these patterns. Once we begin the diagramming, the patterns and terms will make sense.

**Pattern #1 - Subject + Verb**

```
   subject  |  verb
_____

    God     |  provides        (The Bible)
_____
```

**Pattern #2 - Subject + Verb + Direct Object**

```
  subject |  verb  | direct object
_____

   God    |  loves |    you           (John 3:16)
_____
```

# Instructions to Student

## Pattern #3 - Subject + Verb + Indirect Object + Direct Object

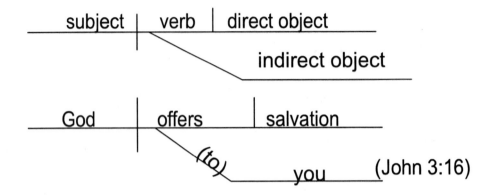

## Pattern # 4 - Subject + Linking Verb + Predicate Complement

```
   subject   |  linking verb \  predicate complement
─────────────┼──────────────────────────────────────
             |
 Holy Spirit |      is       \      God      (Genesis 1:2)
─────────────┼──────────────────────────────────────
             |
```

## Pattern # 5 - Subject + Linking Verb + Predicate Adjective

```
   subject   |  linking verb \  predicate adjective
─────────────┼──────────────────────────────────────
             |
    God      |      is       \    timeless    (Psalm 102:12, 25-27)
─────────────┼──────────────────────────────────────
             |
```

## Instructions to Student

Now you are ready to begin diagramming sentences. You will use the five patterns that you have learned. You will practice each new diagramming model until you have mastered the concept.

The **subject + verb pattern** divides a simple sentence between the subject and predicate. Look at the first example on page 6. Notice that the entire thought is in bold letters. Next, notice that there is a vertical line drawn between the subject and the predicate. This diagram merely draws a picture around and between the words of the sentence to divide its separate parts.

The first five sentences are diagrammed for you on page 6 to give further examples of this beginning formula. Your teacher may review other examples with you.

Read the instructions on page 7 for diagramming the **subject + verb pattern.** Then on page 8 **rewrite the words in dark print onto the blank diagrams. Words in dark print are being**

## Instructions to Student

**studied in the current lesson**. In later lessons you will have underlined words as well as words in bold type. <u>Underlined words are words that have been studied in previous lessons</u> and need to be included in your diagrams. Words that are not in dark print or underlined will be studied in future lessons.

The teacher may go over one or more of these practice sentences out loud in class. If you are unsure of how to diagram these sentences, ask your teacher before going on to the next set of sentences.

Next, after reading the instructions for the test sentences on page 9, copy one sentence at a time (page 10). **Copy all the words in dark print**. Then you will draw the lines to diagram each sentence. Write each of the words in the appropriate place on the diagram.

A test over each unit will reinforce what you have learned in the previous lessons.

# Contents

## Unit 1
## Diagramming Parts of Speech and Sentence Patterns

Title

1. Recognizing Nouns.................................................................. 2
2. Recognizing Action Verbs......................................................... 3
3. **Diagramming Subject-Verb Sentence Pattern** ............... 4
4. Recognizing Helping Verbs ......................................................11
5. Recognizing Pronouns ............................................................12
6. **Diagramming Subject-Verb-Direct Object Sentence Pattern** ............................................................... 17
7. **Diagramming Subject-Verb-Indirect Object-Direct Object Sentence Pattern**................................. 25
8. Recognizing Linking Verbs....................................................... 33
9. **Diagramming Subject-Linking Verb-Predicate Complement Sentence Pattern**.................34
10. Recognizing Adjectives............................................................41
11. **Diagramming Subject-Linking Verb-Predicate Adjective Sentence Pattern**......................... 43
12. **Diagramming Subject "You" Understood Sentence Pattern** ..............................................................50
13. Unit 1 - Test...........................................................................55

# Unit 2
## Diagramming More Parts of Speech and Verbals

### Title

| | | |
|---|---|---|
| 14. | Diagramming Prepositions | 57 |
| 15. | Diagramming Direct Adjectives | 66 |
| 16. | Diagramming Participles | 72 |
| 17. | Recognizing Adverbs | 80 |
| 18. | Diagramming Adverbs | 81 |
| 19. | Diagramming Interjections | 88 |
| 20. | Diagramming Conjunctions | 93 |
| 21. | Diagramming Pronouns | 104 |
| 22. | Diagramming Infinitives | 113 |
| 23. | Diagramming Gerunds | 124 |
| 24. | Diagramming Appositives | 134 |
| 25. | Diagramming Nouns of Address | 142 |
| **26.** | **Unit 2 - Test** | **150** |

# Unit 3
## Diagramming Clauses

| | | |
|---|---|---|
| 27. | Diagramming Noun Clauses | 152 |
| 28. | Diagramming Adjective Clauses | 164 |
| 29. | Diagramming Adverb Clauses | 173 |
| **30.** | **Unit 3 - Test** | **184** |

# Unit 4
# Diagramming Types of Sentences

## Title

| | | |
|---|---|---|
| 31. | Diagramming Simple Sentences | 186 |
| 32. | Diagramming Compound Sentences | 193 |
| 33. | Diagramming Complex Sentences | 200 |
| **34.** | **Unit 4 - Test** | **212** |

## Unit 5

| | | |
|---|---|---|
| 35. | All Units - Test | 213 |

## Answers

| | **Unit 1** | Practice | Test |
|---|---|---|---|
| 3. | Subject - Verb Pattern | 217 | 218 |
| 6. | Subject - Verb - Direct Object Pattern | 219 | 220 |
| 7. | Subject - Verb - Indirect Object - Direct Object Pattern | 221 | 222 |
| 9. | Subject - Linking Verb - Predicate Complement Pattern | 223 | 224 |
| 11. | Subject - Linking Verb - Predicate Adjective Pattern | 225 | 226 |
| 12. | "You" Understood Sentences | 227 | 228 |
| **13.** | **Unit 1 - Test** | | **229** |

| | **Unit 2** | Practice | Test |
|---|---|---|---|
| 14. | Prepositional Phrases | 230 | 232 |
| 15. | Direct Adjectives | 234 | 236 |
| 16. | Participles | 238 | 240 |
| 17. | Recognizing Adverbs | 241 | |
| 18. | Adverbs | 242 | 244 |
| 19. | Interjections | 246 | 247 |
| 20. | Conjunctions | 248 | 251 |
| 21. | Pronouns | 253 | 256 |
| 22. | Infinitives | 258 | 260 |
| 23. | Gerunds | 263 | 266 |
| 24. | Appositives | 268 | 270 |
| 25. | Nouns of Direct Address | 272 | 274 |
| **26.** | **Unit 2 - Test** | | **276** |

| | **Unit 3** | | |
|---|---|---|---|
| 27. | Noun Clauses | 279 | 282 |
| 28. | Adjective Clauses | 285 | 287 |
| 29. | Adverb Clauses | 289 | 292 |
| **30.** | **Unit 3 - Test** | | **295** |

| | **Unit 4** | Practice | Test |
|---|---|---|---|
| 31. | Simple Sentences | 298 | 300 |
| 32. | Compound Sentences | 302 | 304 |
| 33. | Complex Sentences | 306 | 309 |
| 34. | **Unit 4 - Test** | | 311 |

**Unit 5**

35. **All Units Test** ............................................. 314

About the Author .................................................. 324

**Glossary** ............................................................ 325

# Unit 1

## Diagramming Parts of Speech and Basic Sentence Patterns

1. Recognizing Nouns ............................................. 2
2. Recognizing Action Verbs .................................. 3
3. Diagramming Subject-Verb Sentence Pattern  4
4. Recognizing Helping Verbs ............................. 11
5. Recognizing Pronouns .................................... 12
6. Diagramming Subject-Verb-Direct Object Sentence Pattern ....................... 17
7. Diagramming Subject-Verb-Indirect Object-Direct Object Sentence Pattern ........... 25
8. Recognizing Linking Verbs ............................. 33
9. Diagramming Subject-Linking Verb-Predicate Complement Sentence Pattern ....... 34
10. Recognizing Adjectives ................................... 41
11. Diagramming Subject-Linking Verb-Predicate Adjective Sentence Pattern ......................................................... 43
12. Diagramming Subject "You" Understood Sentence Pattern ................................................ 50
13. Unit 1 - Test ..................................................... 55

## 1 - Recognizing Nouns

**Nouns** are parts of speech (words) that name persons, places, things, or qualities. Common nouns name no specific person, place, thing or quality. Proper nouns name a particular person, place, thing or quality. Proper nouns are capitalized.

The following **nouns** are found in the Bible:

| People | Places | Things | Qualities |
|---|---|---|---|
| **Jesus** | **Bethlehem** | sheep | courage |
| shepherd | Galilee | arrow | love |
| disciple | mountain | rock | mercy |
| wife | Samaria | gold | hope |
| David | desert | harp | faith |

**Nouns** are often preceded by the words *a, an,* or *the.* They are called **noun** markers or articles.

In the examples for the subject - verb sentence pattern, **nouns** are used as subjects. In other lessons, nouns will assume other sentence functions and positions.

## 2 - Recognizing Action Verbs

**Action verbs** are words that show action. They tell what the subject does, did or will do.

The following are **action verbs**:

| | | | | | |
|---|---|---|---|---|---|
| suffereth | exalt | make | keep | uphold | borrow |
| provide | shine | obey | rejoices | reveal | knoweth |

Notice that some of these **verbs** end in the suffix *eth* since they are taken from the King James Version of the Bible.

To determine whether a word is a **verb** or not, put *I*, *you*, *he*, or *it* before the word you are checking. If the combination makes a sensible sentence, the word can be a verb. Notice the following:

    I sheep    he sheeps    you sheep    it sheeps

    I heart    he hearts    you heart    it hearts

All of these words are nouns (names) and cannot be used as **verbs**.

Some words can be used as either a noun or a **verb**. A part of speech in a sentence is determined by the job it does in the sentence. When it does the work of a noun, it is a noun: "God is *love*" (1 John 4:8b). When it does the work of a **verb**, it is a **verb**: "*Love* not the world, neither the things that are in the world" (1 John 2:15a).

## 3 - Diagramming Subject + Verb Sentence Pattern

A sentence is a group of words that makes a complete thought. Each sentence has two parts. One part is the naming part or the **subject**. The parts of speech that can be **subjects** are nouns and pronouns. The second part tells what the **subject** is doing or something about the subject. It is called the predicate. It contains the **verb**, a word that shows action or state of being.

In the examples for **subject + verb sentence pattern**, nouns and action verbs are used for subjects and verbs.

| Naming Part | Telling Part |
|---|---|
| God | provides |
| Adam | sinned |
| Eve | sinned |
| Cain | disobeyed |
| Abel | obeyed |

# Diagramming Subject + Verb Sentence Pattern

To decide what words are **verbs** in the examples, look for the action words in the sentences. Another way to decide whether a word is a **verb** or not, use *I, you,* or *he* before it. If it makes good sense, then it is a verb.

Verb Tester

| I music | I sing | I loudly |
| --- | --- | --- |
| you music | you sing | you loudly |
| he music | he sings | he loudly |

To find the **subjects** in the examples, ask "Who?" or "What?" <u>before</u> the **verbs**.

Who provides? God    Who disobeyed? Cain

Who sinned? Adam    Who obeyed? Abel

Who sinned? Eve

# Diagramming Subject + Verb Sentence Pattern
## Examples

1. **God provides.** (The Bible)

```
    God    |    provides
_____|_____
           |
```

2. **Adam sinned.** (Genesis 3:6)

```
   Adam    |    sinned
_____|_____
           |
```

3. **Eve sinned.** (Genesis 3:6)

```
    Eve    |    sinned
_____|_____
           |
```

4. **Cain disobeyed.** (Genesis 4:3-8)

```
   Cain    |    disobeyed
_____|_____
           |
```

5. **Abel obeyed.** (Genesis 4:4)

```
   Abel    |    obeyed
_____|_____
           |
```

## Diagramming Subject + Verb Sentence Pattern
Directions for Practice Sheets

For each sentence, do the following:

1. Find the action word. The answer is the **verb**. Place that word to the right of the vertical line.

2. Ask "Who?" or "What?" before the **verb.** The answer is the **subject**. Place that word to the left of the vertical line that goes through the horizontal line.

# Diagramming Subject + Verb Sentence Pattern
## Practice Sheet

1. **Abraham tithed.** (Genesis 14:20)

2. **Sarah laughed.** (Genesis 18:12)

3. **Hagar fled.** (Genesis 16:6)

4. **Isaac married.** (Genesis 24:67)

5. **Esau bargained.** (Genesis 25:33)

## Diagramming Subject + Verb Sentence Pattern
Directions for Test

1. Draw a horizontal line.

2. Place the **subject** on the left of the line.

3. After the **subject**, place a vertical line through the horizontal line equal in length above and below it.

4. Place the **verb** on the horizontal line after the vertical line.

The words in dark type are always to be included in your diagramming. Capitalize any capitalized words. This includes the first word of the sentence.

```
     subject  |  verb
    _____|_____
              |
```

## Diagramming Subject + Verb Sentence Pattern
Test

1. **Jacob lied**. (Genesis 27:19)

2. **Joseph forgave**. (Genesis 50:16-21)

3. **Judah compromised**. (Genesis 37:26-27)

4. **Moses fasted**. (Exodus 34:28)

5. **Aaron obeyed**. (Exodus 7:6)

## 4 - Recognizing Helping Verbs

**Helping verbs** may be used with main verbs in sentences.

They may be separated from the main verb by the word "not."

Example: "Thou shalt not steal" (Exodus 20:19).

The underlined verbs also may be used as main verbs.

For example: "<u>Do</u> all in the name of the Lord Jesus" (Colossians 3:17b). The subject "you" is understood in this sentence.

| <u>am</u> | <u>have</u> | <u>do</u> | can | will | shall | may |
|---|---|---|---|---|---|---|
| <u>is</u> | <u>has</u> | <u>does</u> | could | would | should | might |
| <u>are</u> | <u>had</u> | <u>did</u> | | | | must |
| <u>was</u> | <u>hath</u> | <u>doth</u> | | | | |
| <u>were</u> | | | | | | |
| <u>be</u> | | | | | | |
| <u>being</u> | | | | | | |
| <u>been</u> | | | | | | |

Memorizing these twenty-five helping verbs would prove very useful in the diagramming of sentences.

# 5 - Recognizing Pronouns

**Pronouns** are words that take the place of nouns. Instead of repeating a noun over and over, **pronouns** are used.

For example: Instead of saying, "The Lord hath made all things for the Lord," the verse is as follows: "The Lord hath made all things for himself," (Proverbs 16:4a).

| **Types of Pronouns** |
|---|

| **Personal Pronouns** |
|---|
| **I, me, my, mine, you, your, yours, ye, thee thy, thine, he, his, him, she, her, hers, it, its, they, their, theirs, them** |

**Personal pronouns** replace nouns that name persons, places, or things.

Sample sentences

    1. Look unto **me**, and be **ye** saved. (Isaiah 45:22a)

    2. Take no thought for **your** life. (Matthew 6:25b)

    3. Fear **thou** not; for **I** am with **thee**. (Isaiah 41:10a)

# Recognizing Pronouns

---

### Indefinite Pronouns

**whatsoever, whosoever, many, all, no one, everyone, neither, none, whoso**

---

**Indefinite pronouns** do not refer to any definite person, place, or thing.

Sample sentences:

1. For **none** of us liveth to himself, and no man dieth to himself. (Romans 14:7)

2. For **whatsoever** is not of faith is sin. (Romans 14:23b)

3. **Whatsoever** ye do in word or deed, do **all** in the name of the Lord Jesus. (Colossians 3:17a)

---

### Reflexive Pronouns

**myself, ourselves, yourself, yourselves, himself, herself, itself, themselves**

---

## Recognizing Pronouns

**Reflexive pronouns** end in the suffix *-self* or *-selves*. These **pronouns** refer to the subject in the sentence.

Sample Sentences

1. For the **LORD** revealed **himself** to Samuel in Shiloh by the word of the LORD. (1 Sam. 3:21b)

2. The **LORD** hath made all things for **himself**. (Proverbs 16:4a)

3. **David** encouraged **himself** in the LORD his God. (1 Samuel 30:6c)

---
### Demonstrative Pronouns

**this, that, these, those**

---

A **demonstrative pronoun** points out a certain person, place, thing or idea.

Sample Sentence

For other foundation can no man lay than **that** is laid, which is Jesus Christ. (1 Corinthians 3:11)

# Recognizing Pronouns

---
**Interrogative Pronouns**

**who, whose, whom, what, which**

---

**Interrogative pronouns** introduce questions.

Sample Sentences

1. For **who** hath known the mind of the Lord, that he may instruct him? (1 Corinthians 2:16a)

2. **Who** knoweth whether thou art come to the kingdom for such a time as this? (Esther 4:14c)

---
**Relative Pronouns**

**who, whosoever, whose, whom, which, that**

---

**Relative pronouns** introduce adjective dependent clauses. A dependent clause is a group of words with a subject and a verb, but it cannot stand by itself. Adjectives modify nouns and pronouns. The dependent clauses are underlined.

## Recognizing Pronouns

Sample Sentences

1. He **that** tilleth his land shall be satisfied with bread. (Proverbs 12:11a)

2. He **that** covereth his sins shall not prosper. (Proverbs 28:13a)

3. He **that** feareth the commandment shall be rewarded. (Proverbs 13:13b)

## 6 - Diagramming <u>Subject</u> + <u>Verb</u> + Direct Object Sentence Pattern

In the <u>subject</u> + <u>verb</u> + **direct object pattern** the subject acts upon something else. The <u>verb</u> is always an action word.

To decide whether a word is a <u>verb</u> or not, use *I, you, he* or *it* before it. If it makes good sense, it is a <u>verb</u>. Notice the <u>verbs</u> in the examples:

    He <u>reproved</u>    He <u>hath remembered</u>    He <u>leadeth</u>

    LORD <u>giveth</u>    He <u>shall feed</u>

After finding the <u>verb</u>, ask "*Who?*" or "*What?*" <u>before</u> it to find the <u>subject</u>.

    Who reproved?  <u>He</u>    Who hath remembered?  <u>He</u>

    Who leadeth?  <u>He</u>    Who giveth?  <u>LORD</u>

    Who shall feed?  <u>He</u>

Notice two <u>action</u> <u>verbs</u> have <u>helping</u> <u>verbs</u>: *shall* and *hath*. They assist the main <u>verb</u>. There may be more than one

## Diagramming <u>Subject</u> + <u>Verb</u> + Direct Object
## Sentence Pattern

<u>helping</u> <u>verb</u> (should have come). Sometimes *not* comes between the <u>verbs</u> (should *not* have come). Memorize the list of <u>helping</u> <u>verbs</u> so that you can easily recognize them (see page 11).

To find the **object** of the <u>verb</u>, say "Whom?" or "What?" <u>after</u> the <u>verb</u>. In a <u>subject</u> + <u>verb</u> + **object sentence pattern**, the word "**object**" always means the **direct object** or the **object** of the <u>action</u> <u>verb</u> in the sentence.

| | |
|---|---|
| He reproved whom? | **kings** |
| He hath remembered what? | **covenant** |
| He leadeth whom? | **me** |
| LORD giveth what? | **wisdom** |
| He shall feed what? | **flock** |

**Direct objects** can be nouns or pronouns. Nouns are words that name persons, places, things or qualities (Lesson 1). A pronoun takes the place of a noun (Lesson 5).

# Diagramming Subject + Verb + Direct Object
## Sentence Pattern
Examples

1. He reproved kings for their sakes. (Psalm 105:14b)

```
   He   |  reproved  |  kings
_____|_____|_____
        |
```

2. He hath remembered his covenant for ever. (Psalm 105:8a)

```
   He   |  hath remembered  |  covenant
_____|_____|_____
        |
```

3. He leadeth me beside the still waters. (Psalm 23:2b)

```
   He   |  leadeth  |  me
_____|_____|_____
        |
```

4. For the LORD giveth wisdom. (Proverbs 2:6a)

```
  LORD  |  giveth  |  wisdom
_____|_____|_____
        |
```

5. He shall feed his flock like a shepherd. (Isaiah 40:11a)

```
   He   |  shall feed  |  flock
_____|_____|_____
        |
```

# Diagramming <u>Subject</u> + <u>Verb</u> + Direct Object
## Sentence Pattern
Directions for Practice Sheet

First, study the examples for the **direct object**. Then study the sentences on the practice sheet.

For each sentence, do the following:

1. Find the action word. The answer is the verb. Place that word in the middle section of the diagram.

2. Ask "Who?" or "What?" *before* the verb. The answer is the subject. Place that word in the first section of the diagram before the vertical line that goes through the horizontal line.

3. Ask "Who?" or "What?" *after* the action word. That answer is the direct object. Place that word after the short vertical line that does not go through the horizontal line.

4. Ignore any words that are not underlined or in dark print.

# Diagramming Subject + Verb + Direct Object
## Sentence Pattern
Practice Sheet

1. A merry <u>heart</u> <u>doeth</u> **good** like a medicine.
   (Proverbs 17:22a)

2. Every wise <u>woman</u> <u>buildeth</u> her **house.** (Proverbs 14:1a)

3. A righteous <u>man</u> <u>regardeth</u> the **life** of his beast.
   (Proverbs 12:10a)

4. The **meek** <u>will</u> <u>he</u> <u>guide</u> in judgment. (Psalm 25:9a)

5. The <u>LORD</u> <u>loveth</u> the **righteous.** (Psalm 146:8c)

## Diagramming <u>Subject</u> + <u>Verb</u> + Direct Object
### Sentence Pattern
Directions for Test

For each sentence, do the following:

1. Draw a horizontal line for the base line.

2. Draw a vertical line to go between the subject and the verb. This line goes all the way through the base line.

3. Draw another vertical line to go between the action verb and the direct object. This line does not go through the horizontal line.

4. Find the action verb. Place it in the center section.

5. For the subject ask "Who?" or "What?" <u>before</u> the action verb. Place it on the left side of the verb.

6. Ask "Who?" or "What?" <u>after</u> the action verb for the **direct object**. Place it on the right side of the verb.

Capitalize any words that are capitalized in the sentence.

Diagram all underlined words and words in dark print. The

# Diagramming <u>Subject</u> + <u>Verb</u> + Direct Object
## Sentence Pattern
Directions for Test

underlined words you have already diagrammed in a previous lesson, and words in dark print are the words presented in this lesson. Ignore words that are not underlined or in dark print. They will be studied in a later lesson.

Example:

noun or pronoun              noun or pronoun

| subject | verb | **direct object** |
|---------|------|-------------------|

## Diagramming <u>Subject</u> + <u>Verb</u> + Direct Object Sentence Pattern

### Test

1. The <u>LORD</u> <u>taketh</u> **pleasure** in his people. (Psalm 149:4a)

2. The <u>LORD</u> <u>openeth</u> the **eyes** of the blind. (Psalm 146:8a)

3. <u>He</u> <u>shall</u> <u>cover</u> **thee** with his feathers. (Psalm 91:4a)

4. <u>He</u> <u>appointed</u> the **moon** for seasons. (Psalm 104:19a)

5. <u>God</u> <u>setteth</u> the **solitary** in families. (Psalm 68:6a)

## 7 - Diagramming <u>Subject</u> + <u>Verb</u> + Indirect Object + Direct Object Sentence Pattern

An **indirect object** is a noun or pronoun (a word that takes the place of a noun) that tells to whom or for whom something is done or given. The words *to* or *for* are <u>not</u> written in the sentence; they are just understood. The **indirect object** comes between the action <u>verb</u> and the <u>direct object</u>.

Directions for example page:

Study each example by finding each of the sentence parts.

**I will give thee money** for the field. (Genesis 23:13c)

Find the <u>verb</u> or action word(s): will give.

Say the word "Who?" *before* the <u>verb</u> for the subject. The answer is "I."

Say the word "What?" *after* the action <u>verb</u> for the <u>direct object</u>. The answer is "money."

Ask "To whom will the money be given?" for the **indirect object**. The word "thee" tells to whom the money will be given.

# Diagramming <u>Subject</u> + <u>Verb</u> + Indirect Object + <u>Direct</u> <u>Object</u> Sentence Pattern

Questions to find **Indirect Objects**

Sentence 2: To whom will I give a drink?   **camels**

Sentence 3: To whom hast thou taught the way?   **them**

Sentence 4: To whom have I given an example?   **you**

Sentence 5: To whom have I given thy word?   **them**


An (x) takes the place of the "understood" *to* or *for*.

# Diagramming <u>Subject</u> + <u>Verb</u> + Indirect Object + <u>Direct Object</u> Sentence Pattern
Examples

1. <u>I</u> <u>will</u> <u>give</u> **thee** <u>money</u> for the field. (Genesis 23:13c)

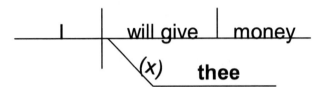

2. <u>I</u> <u>will</u> <u>give</u> thy **camels** <u>drink</u> also. (Genesis 24:14b)

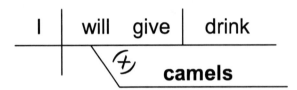

3. <u>Thou</u> <u>hast</u> <u>taught</u> **them** the good <u>way</u>. (2 Chronicles 6:27c)

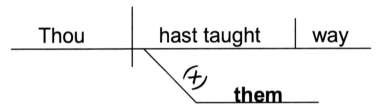

4. For <u>I</u> <u>have</u> <u>given</u> **you** an <u>example</u>. (John 13:15a)

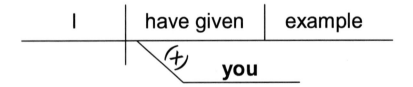

5. <u>I</u> <u>have</u> <u>given</u> **them** thy <u>word</u>. (John 17:14a)

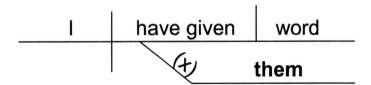

# Diagramming <u>Subject</u> + <u>Verb</u> + Indirect Object + <u>Direct Object</u> Sentence Pattern
## Directions for Practice Sheet

1. Find the action word. The answer is the verb. Place that word in the middle section of the diagram.

2. Ask "Who?" or "What?" *before* the verb. The answer is the subject. Place that word in the first section of the diagram before the vertical line that goes through the horizontal line.

3. Ask "Who?" or "What?" *after* the action word. That answer is the direct object. Place that word after the short vertical line that does not go through the horizontal line.

4. Ask "To whom?" or "For whom is something done?" Place that word on the horizontal line beneath the verb.

5. Put (x) on slanted line attached to indirect object to show that "to" or "for" is understood.

# Diagramming Subject + Verb + Indirect Object + Direct Object Sentence Pattern
Practice Sheet

1. The God of Israel grant thee thy petition. (1 Samuel 1:17b)

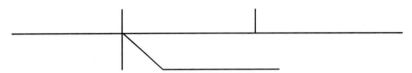

2. I will pay thee my vows. (Psalm 66:13b)

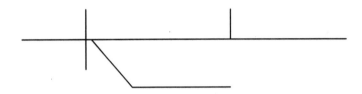

3. I will give you the sure mercies of David. (Acts 13:34b)

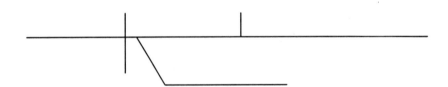

4. I made me great works. (Ecclesiastes 2:4a)

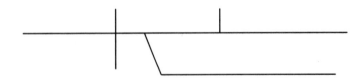

5. The king granted him all his request. (Ezra 7:6c)

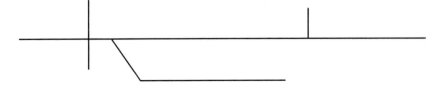

# Diagramming <u>Subject</u> + <u>Verb</u> + Indirect Object + <u>Direct</u> <u>Object</u> Sentence Pattern
## Directions for Test

For each sentence, do the following:

1. Draw a horizontal line for the base line.

2. Draw a vertical line to go between the subject and the verb. This line goes all the way through the base line.

3. Draw another vertical line to go between the action verb and the direct object. This line does not go through the horizontal line.

4. Find the action verb. Place it in the center section.

5. For the subject, ask "Who?" or "What?" *before* the action verb. Place it on the left side of the verb.

6. Ask "Who?" or "What?" *after* the action verb for the direct object. Place it on the right side of the verb.

7. Ask "To whom?" or "For whom is something done?" for the **indirect object**. Place that word on the

# Diagramming <u>Subject</u> + <u>Verb</u> + Indirect Object + **Direct Object** Sentence Pattern
Directions for Test

horizontal line under the verb. Put (x) on the slanted line connecting the verb to the **indirect object**.

Capitalize any words that are capitalized in the sentence. Diagram all underlined words and words in dark print. The underlined words you have already diagrammed in a previous lesson, and words in dark print are the words presented in this lesson. Ignore words that are not underlined or in dark print. They will be studied in a later lesson.

Example:

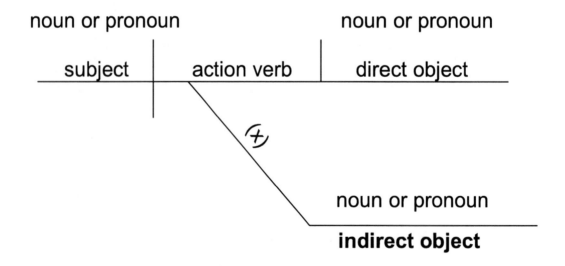

# Diagramming Subject + Verb + Indirect Object + Direct Object Sentence Pattern
Test

1. I have provided **me** a king among his sons. (1 Samuel 16:1d)

2. Thou shalt not make **thee** any graven image.

   (Deuteronomy 5:8a)

3. The LORD will build **thee** an house. (1 Chronicles 17:10c)

4. He shall send **them** a saviour. (Isaiah 19:20c)

5. God will provide **himself** a lamb for a burnt offering.

   (Genesis 22:8a)

## 8 - Recognizing Linking Verbs

**Linking verbs** are words that express a state of being or condition of existence. These words tell what the subject is, was, or will be. They connect the subject to a word that renames it or describes it. In a subject + **linking verb** + complement sentence pattern, a noun or a pronoun renames the subject. An equal sign (=) could replace the **linking verb**. They do not show any action.

### Linking Verbs

| am  | was  | will be   | has been  | had been        |
| is  | were | shall be  | have been | shall have been |
| are | be   | being     | become    | will have been  |

## 9 - Diagramming <u>Subject</u> + Linking Verb + Predicate Complement Sentence Pattern

In this pattern the **linking verb** connects the subject to another noun or pronoun after the **linking verb**. The **linking verb** shows no action. An equal sign (=) could be put in its place.

Study the list of **linking verbs**. Memorizing them will prove to be very helpful.

Directions: Study the examples. Find the word(s) in the sentences that rename the <u>subjects</u>.

Examples:

| <u>Subject</u> | | <u>Complement</u> |
|---|---|---|
| Eve | = | help |
| Methuselah | = | one |

Notice the slanted line between the **linking verb** and the complement (noun or pronoun). It slants backwards toward the <u>subject</u>. It does not go below the horizontal line.

# Diagramming <u>Subject</u> + Linking Verb + Predicate Complement Sentence Pattern
## Examples

1. <u>Eve</u> **was** Adam's **help** meet. (Genesis 2:20-23)

   ```
   Eve    |  was  \  help
   ─────────────────────────
          |
   ```

2. <u>Methuselah</u> **became one** of the oldest men. (Genesis 5:27)

   ```
   Methuselah  |  became  \  one
   ──────────────────────────────
               |
   ```

3. <u>Noah</u> **became** an **heir** of the righteousness which is by faith. (Hebrews 11:7)

   ```
   Noah   |  became  \  heir
   ─────────────────────────
          |
   ```

4. <u>Abraham</u> **was** a **sojourner** in the land of promise. (Hebrews 11:9)

   ```
   Abraham  |  was  \  sojourner
   ──────────────────────────────
            |
   ```

5. <u>Sarah</u> **became** a **mother** of nations. (Genesis 17:16b)

   ```
   Sarah  |  became  \  mother
   ───────────────────────────
          |
   ```

# Diagramming Subject + Linking Verb + Predicate Complement Sentence Pattern
## Directions for Practice Sheet

For each sentence, do the following:

1. Find the **linking verb**. Place that word in the middle section of the diagram.

2. Ask "Who?" or "What?" before the **linking verb**. The answer is the subject. Place that word in the first section of the diagram before the vertical line that goes through the horizontal line.

3. Ask "Who?" or "What?" after the **linking verb**. That answer is the **predicate complement**. The line slants back to the subject because the **predicate complement** is the same as the subject. Place that word(s) after the slanting line.

# Diagramming Subject + Linking Verb + Predicate Complement Sentence Pattern
## Practice Sheet

1. I **am** the **door.** (John 10:9a)

2. I **am** the true **vine.** (John 15:1a)

3. I **am** the living **bread.** (John 6:51a)

4. This **is** my beloved **Son.** (Luke 9:35b)

5. He **was** a burning and a shining **light.** (John 5:35a)

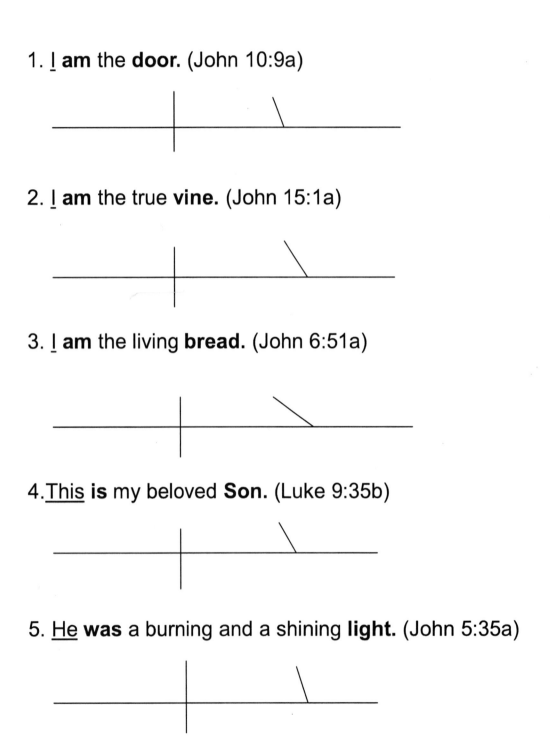

# Diagramming <u>Subject</u> + Linking Verb + Predicate Complement Sentence Pattern
## Directions for Test

For each sentence, do the following:

1. Draw a horizontal line for the base line.

2. Draw a vertical line to go between the <u>subject</u> and the **linking verb**. This line goes all the way through the base line.

3. Draw a slanting line to go between the **linking verb** and the **predicate complement**. This line does not go through the horizontal line.

4. Find the **linking verb.** Place it in the center section.

5. For the <u>subject</u>, ask "Who?" or "What?" before the **linking verb**. Place that word on the left side of the **linking verb**.

6. For the **predicate complement,** find the word that renames the <u>subject</u> after the **linking verb**. Place it on the right side of the slanting line.

# Diagramming <u>Subject</u> + Linking Verb + Predicate Complement Sentence Pattern
## Directions for Test

Capitalize any words that are capitalized in the sentence. Diagram all underlined words and words in dark print. The underlined words you have already diagrammed in a previous lesson, and the words in dark print are the words presented in this lesson. Ignore any words that are not underlined or in dark print. They will be studied in a later lesson.

Example:

noun or pronoun                                         noun or pronoun

subject | **linking verb** \ **complement**

## Diagramming Subject + Linking Verb + Predicate Complement Sentence Pattern
Test

1. The <u>LORD</u> **is** my **shepherd**. (Psalm 23:1a)

2. <u>Sin</u> **is** the **transgression** of the law. (1 John 3:4b)

3. <u>We</u> **are labourers** together with God.

   (1 Corinthians 3:9a)

4. <u>Ye</u> **are** God's **husbandry**. (1 Corinthians 3:9b)

5. <u>Ye</u> **are** God's **building**. (1 Corinthians 3:9c)

# 10 - Recognizing Adjectives

**Adjectives** are words that modify or limit nouns or pronouns. They usually precede the word that they modify, but they may come after a linking verb and describe the subject. They answer certain questions as shown in the chart below.

| What <u>Color</u>? | What <u>Size</u>? | What <u>kind</u>? |
|---|---|---|
| **blue** clothes | **small** cloud | **parched** ground |
| **green** herb | **short** time | **sufficient** grace |
| **gray** hairs | **broad** walls | **abundant** grace |
| **black** horse | **tall** cedars | **perfect** strength |

| Which <u>one(s)</u>? | <u>Whose</u>? | How <u>many</u>? |
|---|---|---|
| **eighth** day | **bird's** nest | **twelve** tribes |
| **southward** side | **his** birthday | **every** sin |
| **fiftieth** year | **thine** adversary | **few** labourers |
| **these** commands | **priest's** robes | **all** nations |

## Recognizing Adjectives

The **adjectives** shown in the chart are direct adjectives. They come before the noun or pronoun that they modify. A **predicate adjective** comes after a linking verb and describes the subject.

The following are examples of sentences which contain **predicate adjectives**:

All the promises of God in him are **yea**.

(2 Corinthians 1:20a)

The Lord is **good.** (Psalm 100:5a)

Possessive pronouns like *his* and *thine* are pronouns because they refer to noun or pronoun antecedents. However, they have the character of adjectives because they modify nouns.

## 11 - Diagramming <u>Subject</u> + <u>Linking</u> <u>Verb</u> + Predicate Adjective Sentence Pattern

In the <u>subject</u> + <u>linking</u> <u>verb</u> + **predicate adjective** sentence pattern the <u>subject</u> is followed by a <u>linking verb</u> and a word which describes the <u>subject</u> instead of renaming it.

Study the chart on **adjectives**. Note the different questions that the **adjectives** answer.

Directions: Study the examples.

1. The **predicate adjective** "**yea**" tells what kind of "promises" (subject - a noun).

2. The **predicate adjective** "**blessed**" tells what kind of "merciful" (subject - a noun).

3. The **predicate adjective** "**kind**" tells what kind of "ye" (subject - a pronoun).

4. The **predicate adjective** "**sufficient**" tells what kind of "grace" (subject - a noun).

5. The **predicate adjective** "**perfect**" tells what kind of "strength" (subject - a noun).

# Diagramming Subject + Linking Verb + Predicate Adjective Sentence Pattern
## Examples

1. All the promises of God in him are yea. (2 Corinthians 1:20a)

   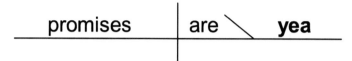

2. **Blessed** are the merciful. (Matthew 5:7a)

   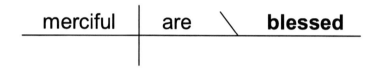

3. Be ye kind one to another. (Ephesians 4:32a)

   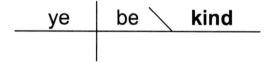

4. My grace is **sufficient** for thee. (2 Corinthians 12:9a)

   grace | is \ **sufficient**

5. My strength is made **perfect** in weakness. (2 Corinthians 12:9b)

   strength | is made \ **perfect**

# Diagramming <u>Subject</u> + <u>Linking Verb</u> + **Predicate Adjective** Sentence Pattern

## Directions for Practice Sheet

For each sentence, do the following:

1. Find the <u>linking verb</u>. Place that word in the middle section of the diagram.

2. Ask "Who?" or "What?" <u>before</u> the <u>linking verb</u>. The answer is the <u>subject</u>. Place that word in the first section of the diagram before the vertical line that goes through the horizontal line.

3. Ask "Who?" or "What?" <u>after</u> the <u>linking verb</u>. That answer is the **predicate adjective**. The line slants back to the <u>subject</u> because the **predicate adjective** describes the <u>subject</u>. Place that word after the slanting line.

# Diagramming Subject + Linking Verb + Predicate Adjective Sentence Pattern

## Practice Sheet

1. The LORD is **good**. (Psalm 135:3b)

2. Jonathan, Saul's son, was **unselfish**. (1 Samuel 18:3-4)

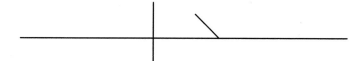

3. Solomon was **wise**. (1 Kings 3:12)

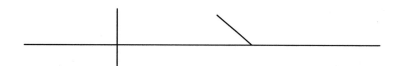

4. Job was **patient**. (James 5:11a)

5. Daniel was **courageous**. (Daniel 1:1-8)

# Diagramming <u>Subject</u> + <u>Linking Verb</u> + Predicate Adjective Sentence Pattern
Directions for Test

For each sentence, do the following:

1. Draw a horizontal line for the base line.

2. Draw a vertical line to go between the <u>subject</u> and the <u>linking verb</u>. This line goes all the way through the base line.

3. Draw a slanting line to go between the <u>linking verb</u> and the **predicate adjective.** This line does not go through the horizontal line.

4. Find the <u>linking verb</u>. Place it in the center section.

5. For the <u>subject</u>, ask "Who?" or "What?" before the <u>linking verb</u>. Place that word on the left side of the <u>linking verb</u>.

6. For the **predicate adjective,** find the word that describes the <u>subject</u> after the <u>linking verb</u>. Place it on the right side of the slanting line.

## Diagramming <u>Subject</u> + <u>Linking Verb</u> + Predicate Adjective Sentence Pattern

## Directions for Test

Diagram all underlined words (words that you have diagrammed in previous lessons) and words in dark print (words presented in this lesson). Ignore any words that are not underlined or in dark print. They will be studied in a later lesson. Capitalize any words that are capitalized in the test sentences.

Example:

noun or pronoun                                             adjective

```
   subject   |   linking verb  \   predicate adjective
_____|_____
             |
```

# Diagramming Subject + Linking Verb + Predicate Adjective Sentence Pattern
## Test

1. Thy testimonies are very **sure**. (Psalm 93:5a)

2. The LORD is **worthy** to be praised. (Psalm 18:3b)

3. Thy mercy is **great** unto the heavens. (Psalm 57:10a)

4. The righteous shall be **glad** in the LORD. (Psalm 64:10a)

5. Esther was **loyal** to God and her people. (Esther 4:15-16)

## 12 - Diagramming Subject "You" Understood Sentence Pattern

Some sentences which give a request or a command have no actual word for the subject. The word "**you**" becomes the understood subject.

Examples:

| Subject | Verb |
|---------|------|
| (you) | **yield** |
| (you) | **follow** |
| (you) | **lift** |
| (you) | **cast** |
| (you) | **abide** |

Directions for Practice Sheet

For each sentence do the following:

1. Find the action word (verb). Place that word on the right side of the first vertical line of the diagram.

2. Ask "Who?" or "What?" before the verb. The answer is "you." Place **(you)** in the first section of the diagram. The word "**you**" is in parentheses since it is understood.

3. Ask "Who?" or "What?" after the action verb. The answer is the direct object. Place it after the short vertical line that does not go through the horizontal line.

# Diagramming Subject "You" Understood Sentence Pattern
## Examples

1. Yield yourselves unto God. (Romans 6:13b)

   | **(you)** | Yield | yourselves |

2. Follow me. (John 1:43c)

   | **(you)** | Follow | me |

3. Lift up your eyes on high. (Isaiah 40:26a)

   | **(you)** | Lift | eyes |

4. Cast thy burden upon the LORD. (Psalm 55:22a)

   | **(you)** | Cast | burden |

5. Abide in me. (John 15:4a)

   | **(you)** | Abide |

# Diagramming Subject "You" Understood Sentence Pattern
## Practice Sheet

1. Search the scriptures. (John 5:39a)

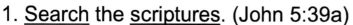

2. Judge not according to the appearance. (John 7:24a)

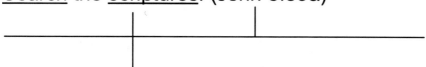

3. Take my yoke upon you. (Matthew 11:29a)

4. Preach the word. (2 Timothy 4:2a)

5. Lord, evermore give us this bread. (John 6:34b)

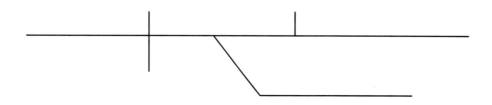

# Diagramming Subject "You" Understood Sentence Pattern
## Directions for Test

For each sentence do the following:

1. Draw a horizontal line for the base line.
2. Draw a vertical line to go between the <u>subject</u> and the <u>verb</u>. This line goes all the way through the base line.
3. Draw another vertical line to go between the action <u>verb</u> and the <u>direct object</u>. This line does not go through the horizontal line.
4. Find the <u>action verb</u> and put it in the center space.
5. Since this sentence is a request, put the <u>subject</u> **"you"** in parentheses in the first section of the diagram.
6. Ask "Who?" or "What?" <u>after</u> the <u>action verb</u> for the <u>direct object</u>. Put it after the vertical line after the <u>verb</u>.

Diagram any word that is underlined or in dark print. Ignore the other words. They will be studied in a later lesson.

Capitalize any words that are capitalized in the sentence.

| (you) | verb | direct object |

# Diagramming Subject "You" Understood Sentence Pattern
Test Sheet

1. <u>Order</u> my <u>steps</u> in thy word. (Psalm 119:133a)

2. <u>Rebuke</u> not an <u>elder</u>. (1 Timothy 5:1a)

3. <u>Come</u> unto me. (Matthew 11:28a)

4. <u>Rejoice</u> in the LORD. (Psalm 33:1a)

5. <u>Deliver</u> <u>me</u> in thy righteousness. (Psalm 71:2a)

## 13 - Unit 1 Test

Directions: Diagram the words in bold type.

1. **God is** our **refuge** and strength, a very present help in trouble. (Psalm 46:1)

2. **Thou shalt make thee** no molten **gods**. (Exodus 34:17)

3. **Remember** the sabbath **day**, to keep it holy. (Exodus 20:8)

4. The **testimony** of the LORD **is sure**, making wise the simple. (Psalm 19:7b)

5. My **soul thirsteth** for God, for the living God. (Psalm 42:2a)

# Unit 2

# Diagramming More Parts of Speech and Verbals

| | | |
|---|---|---|
| 14. | Diagramming Prepositions | 57 |
| 15. | Diagramming Direct Adjectives | 66 |
| 16. | Diagramming Participles | 72 |
| 17. | Recognizing Adverbs | 80 |
| 18. | Diagramming Adverbs | 81 |
| 19. | Diagramming Interjections | 88 |
| 20. | Diagramming Conjunctions | 93 |
| 21. | Diagramming Pronouns | 104 |
| 22. | Diagramming Infinitives | 113 |
| 23. | Diagramming Gerunds | 124 |
| 24. | Diagramming Appositives | 134 |
| 25. | Diagramming Nouns of Address | 142 |
| 26. | Unit 2 - Test | 150 |

## 14 - Diagramming Prepositions

A **preposition** is a word that shows a relationship between its object and another word in the sentence.

Examples:

**By** grace are ye saved **through** faith. (Ephesians 2:8a)

These two **prepositions** introduce phrases that tell us how individuals are saved: *By grace* and *through faith.* Both **prepositional phrases** are used as adverbs because they modify the verb *are saved*.

Fight the good fight **of** faith. (1 Timothy 6:12a)

The word *of* introduces a **prepositional phrase** that modifies the noun *fight*, the word in front of it. As a result, it is an **adjectival prepositional phrase**. It tells us what kind of fight that we are to fight.

**Prepositional phrases** always **begin with a preposition and end with an object**. There may be modifiers between them: "under *a fig* tree," "in *all his* ways," and "with *all thy* heart."

## Diagramming Prepositions

Other **common prepositions** are as follows: **above, after, around, before, beside, between, by, down, for, from, in, of, on, over, to, toward, under, until, up, upon, with.**

**Object pronouns** are always used after a **preposition**. The following are object pronouns: **me, us, her, him, them, whom.**

Study the rest of the examples. Locate the **prepositional phrases** in bold type. Ask what question is answered by the phrase: *which one? whose? how? when?* Ask what word(s) does the **prepositional phrase** modify? The answer you get determines what the phrase modifies and whether it is used as an adverb or an adjective.

See example 5 on page 60 for an example of a prepositional phrase used as a noun. A prepositional phrase used as a noun is called a *nominal*. The *nominal* here comes after the verb *to be* and is a predicate noun.

# Diagramming Prepositions
## Examples

1. **By grace** <u>are</u> <u>ye</u> <u>saved</u> **through faith**. (Ephesians 2:8a)

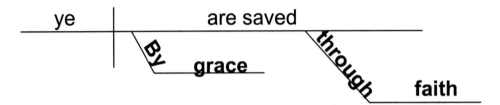

2. <u>Fight</u> the good <u>fight</u> **of faith**. (1 Timothy 6:12a)

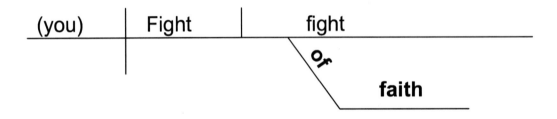

3. <u>I</u> <u>saw</u> <u>thee</u> **under** the fig **tree**. (John 1:50a)

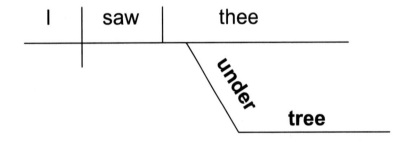

## Diagramming Prepositions
Examples

4. He went up **into** a **mountain**. (Matthew 5:1a)

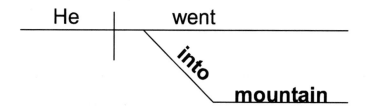

5. No unrighteousness is **in him**. (John 7:18c)

Jesus is speaking of Himself here.

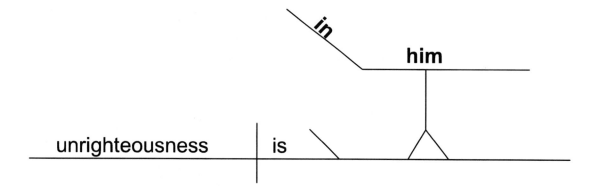

# Diagramming Prepositions
## Directions for Practice Pages

For each sentence, do the following for **prepositional phrases**:

1. Find a word that shows a relationship between its object and another word in the sentence. Refer to the list of **prepositions**.
2. Decide what word the **prepositional phrase** modifies.
3. Place the **preposition** on the slanted line below the modified word.
4. Place the object of the **preposition** on the horizontal line attached to the slanted line.

Example:

Humble yourselves **in** the **sight of** the **Lord**, and he shall lift you up. (James 4:10)

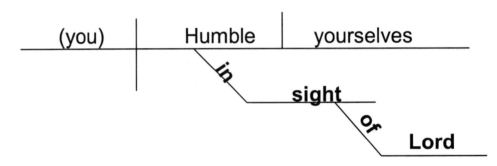

Complete the practice sheets.

# Diagramming Prepositions
## Practice Sheet

1. Be not wise in your own conceits. (Romans 12:16c)

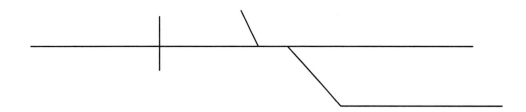

2. Love worketh no ill to his neighbour. (Romans 13:10a)

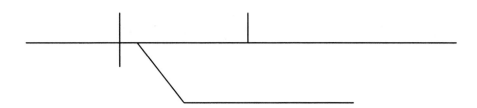

3. Pray without ceasing. (1 Thessalonians 5:17)

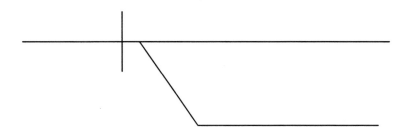

## Diagramming Prepositions
Practice Sheet

4. **In** every **thing** give thanks. (1 Thessalonians 5:18a)

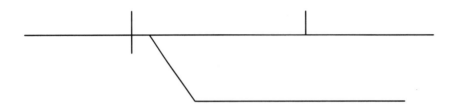

5. They parted my garments among them. (Matthew 27:35b)

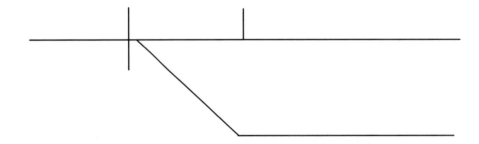

# Diagramming Prepositions
## Directions for Test

For each sentence, do the following for **prepositions**:

1. Find the word that shows a relationship between its object and another word in the sentence.
2. Ask what question is answered by one of the phrases: *which one? whose? how? when? where?*
3. Ask what word(s) does the **prepositional phrase** modify?
4. Draw a slanted line under the word(s) that is modified.
5. Place the **preposition** on this line.
6. Attach a horizontal line to the slanted line.
7. Place the object of the **preposition** on this line.

Example:

The <u>coming</u> **of** the **Lord** <u>draweth</u> nigh. (James 5:8b)

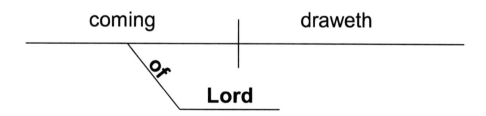

Diagram the test sentences.

## Diagramming Prepositions
Test

1. The <u>love</u> **of money** <u>is</u> the <u>root</u> **of** all **evil**. (1 Timothy 6:10a)

2. A double minded <u>man</u> <u>is unstable</u> **in** all his **ways**.

   (James 1:8)

3. <u>Follow</u> **after charity**. (1 Corinthians 14:1a)

4. The <u>love</u> **of Christ** <u>constraineth</u> <u>us</u>. (2 Corinthians 5:14a)

5. <u>I</u> <u>am</u> <u>crucified</u> **with Christ**: nevertheless I live; yet not I, but

   Christ liveth in me: and the life which I now live in the flesh I

   live by the faith of the Son of God, who loved me, and gave

   himself for me. (Galatians 2:20)

## 15 - Diagramming Direct Adjectives

As you recall, **adjectives** are words that describe nouns and pronouns. Review the material on **adjectives** (page 41).

Study the examples and decide what question each **adjective** answers and what it modifies.

1. Which vine?   **the** vine

   What kind of vine?   **true** vine

2. Which bread?   **the** bread

   What kind of bread?   **living** bread

3. Whose father?   **My** father

   Which husbandman?   **the** husbandman

4. Whose son?   **My** son

   What kind of Son?   **beloved**

5. What light?   **a** light

   What kind of light?   **burning** light

   What kind of light?   **shining** light

### Directions for Practice Sheet

For each diagram, do the following for **adjectives**:

1. Find the **adjectives**, word(s) that describe nouns.

2. Place the **adjectives** on the slanted lines beneath the nouns that they modify.

3. Fill in the diagrams on the practice sheets.

# Diagramming Direct Adjectives
## Examples

1. I am **the true** vine. (John 15:1)

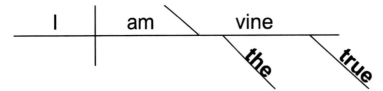

2. I am **the living** bread. (John 6:51a)

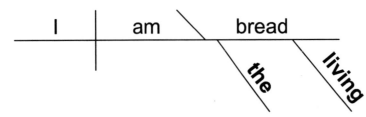

3. **My** father is **the** husbandman. (John 15:1b)

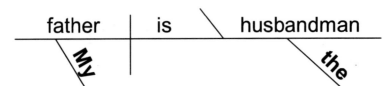

4. This is **my beloved** Son. (Luke 9:35b)

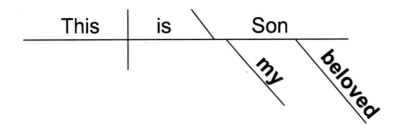

5. He was **a burning** and **a shining** light. (John 5:35a)

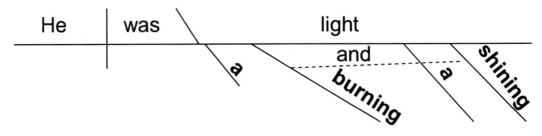

# Diagramming Direct Adjectives
Practice Sheet

1. Ye are **God's** building. (1 Corinthians 3:9c)

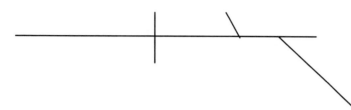

2. **The parched** ground shall become **a** pool. (Isaiah 35:7a)

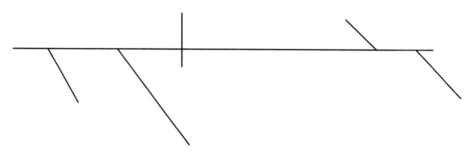

3. **The** words of **the** LORD are **pure** words. (Psalm 12:6a)

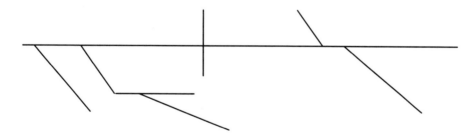

4. Thou art **my hiding** place. (Psalm 32:7a)

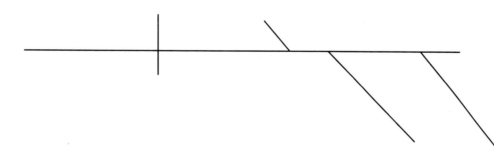

## Diagramming Direct Adjectives
### Practice Sheet

5. **A virtuous** woman is **a** crown to **her** husband.
   (Proverbs 12:4a)

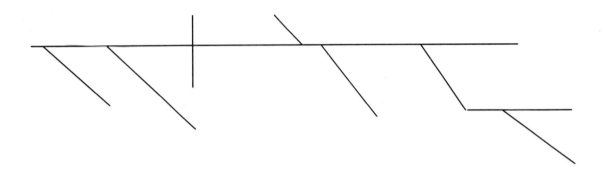

# Diagramming Direct Adjectives
## Directions for Test

For **direct adjectives,** do the following:

1. A **direct adjective** is one that precedes the word it modifies or describes. Draw a slanted line beneath each noun for each **adjective**.
2. Place the **direct adjective** on that line.

For **predicate adjectives** (page 34) you did the following:

1. A **predicate adjective** comes *after* a linking verb and describes the subject. Draw a slanted line after the linking verb on the horizontal line. It points back to the subject.
2. Place the **predicate adjective** after the slanted line.

Example for **direct adjective** and **predicate adjective**:

**My** <u>grace</u> <u>is</u> **sufficient** <u>for</u> <u>thee</u>. (2 Corinthians 12:9a)

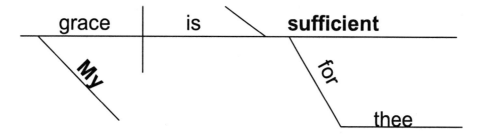

3. Diagram the sentences.

## Diagramming Direct Adjectives
Test

1. I hate **every false** way. (Psalm 119:104b)

2. I have loved thee with **an everlasting** love. (Jeremiah 31:3b)

3. Make **no** friendship with **an angry** man. (Proverbs 22:24a)

4. **His merciful** kindness is great toward us. (Psalm 117:2a)

5. **The just** man walketh in **his** integrity. (Proverbs 20:7a)

## 16 - Diagramming Participles

**Participles** are verbal adjectives. In form they are verbs; in usage they are adjectives. **Present participles** end in "ing." The **past participle** is the third principal part of the verb, as in "break," "broke," "broken."

Directions: Study the example sentences.

1. "**Broken**" is a **participle**, describing the noun "heart."

2. "**Working**" is a **participle**, describing the noun "tongue."

3. "**Hiding**" is a **participle**, describing the noun "place."

4. "**Rejoicing**" is a **participle,** describing the pronoun "I."

5. "**Prating**" is a **participle**, describing the noun "fool."

**Participles** can be modified by adverbs: "deceitfully working," "always rejoicing." Prepositional phrases can also modify **participles**: "like a sharp razor" modifies "working."

# Diagramming Participles
## Examples

1. A **broken** and a contrite heart, O God, thou wilt not despise. (Psalm 51:17b)

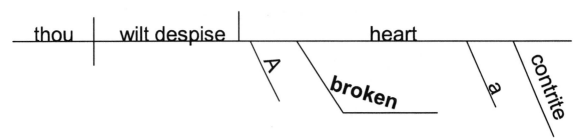

2. Thy tongue deviseth mischiefs; like a sharp razor, **working** deceitfully. (Psalm 52:2)

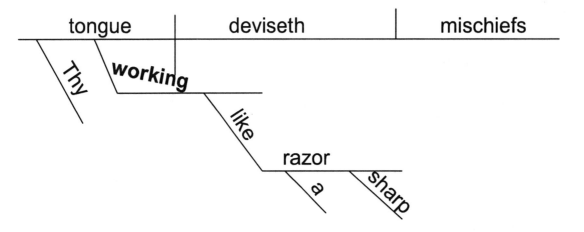

3. Thou art my **hiding** place and my shield. (Psalm 119:114a)

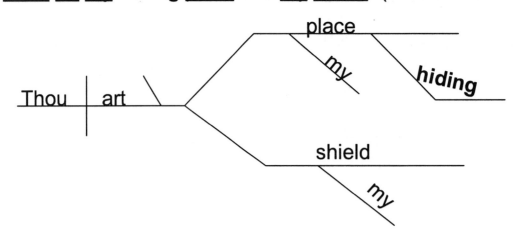

## Diagramming Participles
Examples

4. I was daily his delight; **rejoicing** always before him. (Proverbs 8:30b)

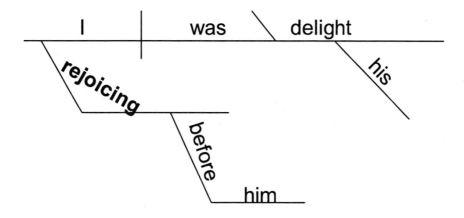

5. The wise in heart will receive commandments: but a **prating** fool shall fall. (Proverbs 10:8)

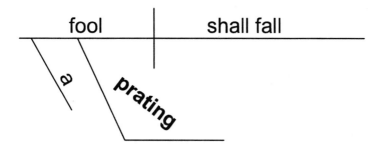

# Diagramming Participles
Directions for Practice Sheets

For each sentence, do the following:

1. Find the word that ends in "ing" or "ed" and is used as an adjective.
2. Slant the **participle** across the structure similar to that of a prepositional phrase.
3. The **participial** structure is below the word that it modifies.

Example:

A **lying** tongue hateth those that are afflicted by it. (Proverbs 26:28b)

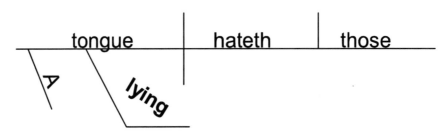

Complete the practice sheets.

Remember the underlined words have been in previous lessons, and the words in bold letters are the **participles.** All the rest of the words will be studied in later lessons.

# Diagramming Participles
## Practice Sheet

1. **Lying** lips are abomination to the LORD. (Proverbs 12:22a)

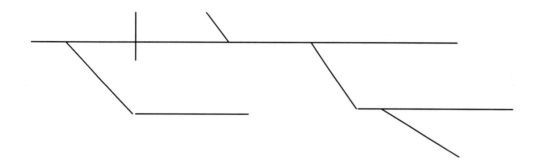

2. Hope **deferred** maketh the heart sick. (Proverbs 13:12a)

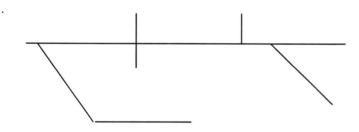

3. From whence then hast thou that **living** water? (John 4:11c)

## Diagramming Participles
### Practice Sheet

4. My son, God will provide himself a lamb for a burnt offering. (Genesis 22:8a)

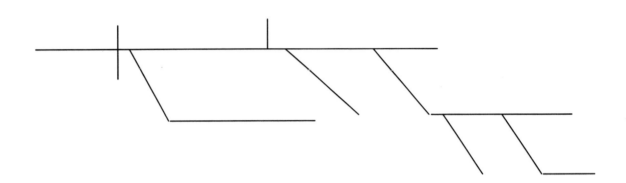

5. When he hath found it, he layeth it on his shoulders, rejoicing. (Luke 15:5)

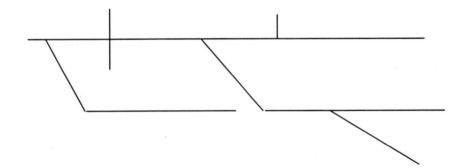

## Diagramming Participles
### Directions for Test

For each sentence, do the following for **participles**:

1. Find the word that ends in "ing" or "ed" and is used as an adjective.
2. Draw a slanted line down from the word that the **participle** modifies.
3. Draw a horizontal line to extend from the slanted line.
4. Slant the **participle** across the structure.
5. If the participle has an object, a short vertical line is drawn between the **participle** and the noun (object).
6. Place prepositional phrases which modify the **participle** underneath the **participle**.

Example:

Ye do err, not **knowing** the scriptures, nor the power of God. (Matthew 22:29)

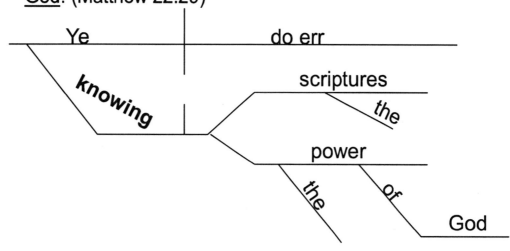

## Diagramming Participles
## Test

1. The child grew, and waxed strong in spirit, **filled** with wisdom.

   (Luke 2:40a)

2. The statutes of the LORD are right, **rejoicing the heart**.

   (Psalm 19:8a)

3. The commandment of the LORD is pure, **enlightening the eyes**. (Psalm 19:8b)

4. The law of the LORD is perfect, **converting the soul**.

   (Psalm 19:7a)

5. The testimony of the LORD is sure, **making** wise **the simple**.

   (Psalm 19:7b)

## 17 - Recognizing Adverbs

An **adverb** is a word that modifies (changes the meaning of) a verb, an adjective, or another **adverb**. **Adverbs** answer these questions: *When? Where? How? To what extent?*

| <u>When</u> Words | <u>Where</u> Words | <u>How</u> Words | <u>How</u> Much Words | |
|---|---|---|---|---|
| then | here | very | wholly | in addition |
| now | aside | gladly | long | |
| first | nigh | quickly | forever | |
| often | away | how | hitherto | |
| today | up | not | daily | |

Verse with **adverb** modifying a <u>verb</u>:

Consider **how** I <u>love</u> thy precepts. (Psalm 119:159)

Verse with **adverb** modifying an <u>adjective</u>:

**How** <u>sweet</u> are thy words unto my taste! (Psalm 119:103a)

Verse with **adverb** modifying another <u>adverb</u>:

I will **very** <u>gladly</u> spend and be spent for you.
(2 Corinthians 12:15a)

## 18 - Diagramming Adverbs

**Adverbs** are words that modify verbs, adjectives, or other **adverbs**. Review the material on **adverbs** before doing this lesson.

Directions:

Study the examples.

1. *Very* modifies *gladly* - tells how gladly.
   *Gladly* modifies *will spend* - tells how.
2. *Also* and *away* modify *will go* - *also* tells in addition and *away* tells where.
3. *Also* modifies *be* - tells in addition.
4. *Again* modifies *must be born* - tells how.
5. *Alway* modifies *rejoice* - tells to what extent.

Notice how compound verbs are diagrammed. They are placed on two different horizontal lines with *and* between them.

### Directions for Practice Sheet

For each diagram, do the following for **adverbs:**

1. Find the **adverbs**, words that modify verbs, adjectives, or other **adverbs**.
2. Place the **adverbs** on the slanted lines beneath the words that they modify.
3. Fill in the diagrams on the practice sheets.

# Diagramming Adverbs
## Examples

1. I will **very gladly** spend and be spent for you. (2 Cor. 12:15a)

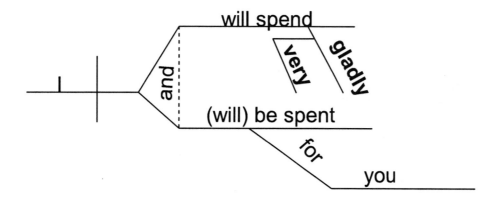

2. Will ye **also** go **away**? (John 6:67b)

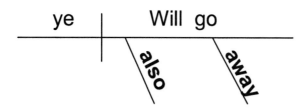

3. Be ye therefore ready **also**. (Luke 12:40a)

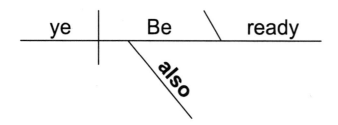

4. Ye must be born **again**. (John 3:7b)

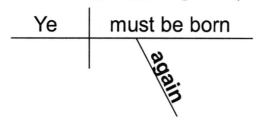

## Diagramming Adverbs
## Examples

5. <u>Rejoice</u> <u>in</u> <u>the</u> <u>Lord</u> **alway**. (Philippians 4:4a)

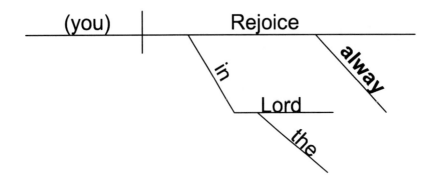

# Diagramming Adverbs
## Practice Sheet

1. **How** sweet are thy words unto my taste! (Psalm 119:103a)

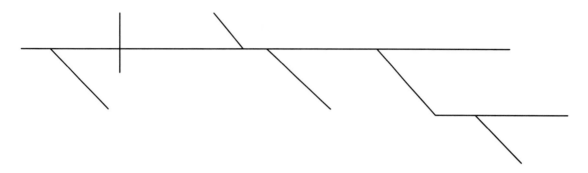

2. I have set the LORD **always** before me. (Psalm 16:8a)

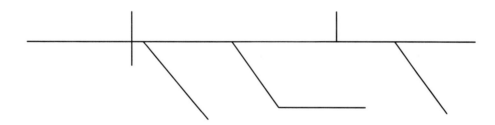

3. Ye can**not** serve God and mammon. (Luke 16:13c)

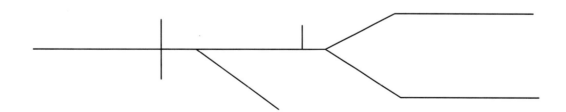

# Diagramming Adverbs
## Practice Sheet

4. Seek ye **first** the kingdom of God, and his righteousness. (Matthew 6:33a)

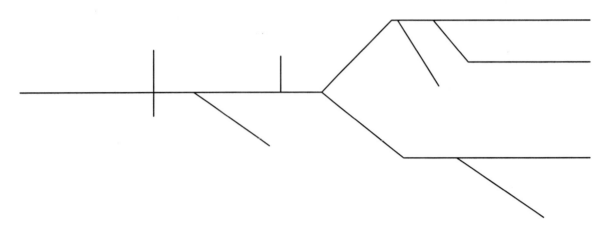

5. In him dwelleth all the fullness of the Godhead **bodily**. (Colossians 2:9)

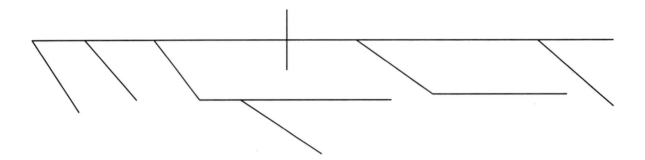

# Diagramming Adverbs
## Directions for Test

To diagram an **adverb,** place it on a slanted line beneath the word(s) that it modifies.

Example:

Will ye **also** go **away**? (John 6:67b)

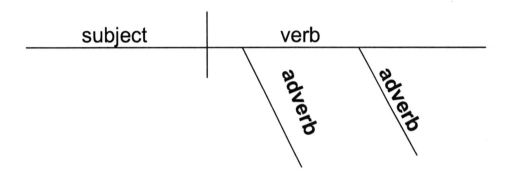

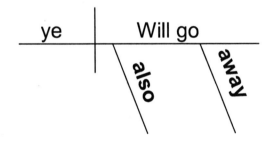

Diagram all the words in the sentences *except* those *not underlined* or in *dark print*. The underlined words have been in previous lessons, and the words in bold letters are the **adverbs**. All the rest of the words will be studied in later lessons.

## Diagramming Adverbs
Test

1. My feet were **almost** gone; my steps had **well nigh** slipped.

   (Psalm 73:2b)

2. The very God of peace sanctify you **wholly**.

   (1 Thessalonians 5:23a)

3. Some have entertained angels **unawares**. (Hebrews 13:2b)

4. Heaven and earth shall pass **away**, but my words shall **not** pass **away**. (Matthew 24:35)

5. Draw **nigh** to God, and he will draw **nigh** to you. (James 4:8a)

# 19 - Diagramming Interjections

**Interjections** are words that show sudden or strong feeling. They are not grammatically connected to the rest of the sentence.

## Common Interjections in the Holy Bible

> **alas, behold, lo, o, yea**

**Interjections** usually come at the beginning of the sentence.

Study the examples. Find the **interjection** and notice that it is not grammatically connected to the rest of the sentence. That is why it is on a separate line above the rest of the sentence.

Directions for Practice Sheets

For each diagram, do the following for **interjections**:

1. Find a word that shows sudden or strong feeling and is not grammatically connected to the rest of the sentence.

2. Place it on the horizontal line above the subject-verb line. Fill in the diagrams on the practice sheets.

Remember the underlined words have been in previous lessons and the words in bold letters are the **interjections**. All the rest of the words will be studied in later lessons.

# Diagramming Interjections
## Examples

1. **Lo**, I come to do thy will, O God. (Hebrews 10:9a)

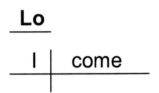

2. **Yea**, I have loved thee with an everlasting love. (Jeremiah 31:3b)

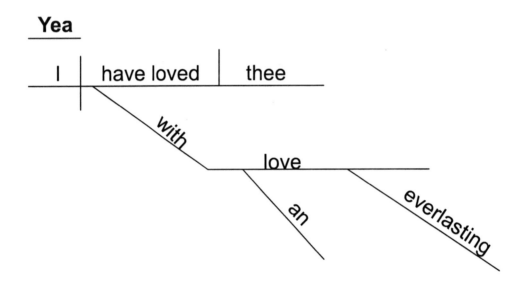

3. **O** how I love thy law! (Psalm 119:97a)

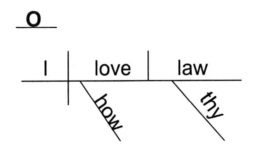

# Diagramming Interjections
## Practice Sheet

1. **Behold,** I stand at the door, and knock. (Revelation 3:20a)

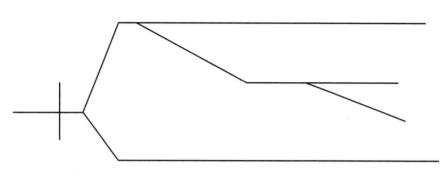

2. **Yea,** I will help thee. (Isaiah 41:10c)

3. **Behold,** what manner of love the Father hath bestowed upon us. (1 John 3:1a)

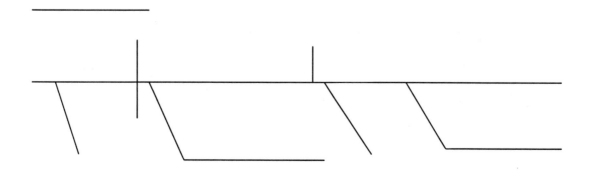

# Diagramming Interjections
## Directions for Test

For each diagram, do the following for **interjections**:

1. Find the word that shows sudden or strong feeling and is not connected grammatically to the rest of the sentence.
2. Place it on a horizontal line to the left above the rest of the sentence.

Example:

**Behold**, I come quickly. (Revelation 22:7a)

| interjection | | **Behold** |
|---|---|---|
| subject | verb | I \| come \\ quickly |

The word *Behold* is capitalized because it is the first word of the sentence.

Remember the underlined words have been in previous lessons, and the words in bold letters are the **interjections**. All the rest of the words will be studied in later lessons.

Diagram the test sentences.

## Diagramming Interjections
### Test

1. **Yea**, I will uphold thee with the right hand of my righteousness.

    (Isaiah 41:10d)

2. **Yea**, happy is that people, whose God is the LORD.

    (Psalm 144:15b)

3. **Behold**, I make all things new. (Revelation 21:5b)

## 20 - Coordinating Conjunctions and Correlative Conjunctions

**Coordinating conjunctions** and **correlative conjunctions** connect words, phrases, and clauses of equal grammatical worth.

> **Coordinating Conjunctions**
>
> **and, but, for, or, so, nor, yet**

Examples: words: James **and** John were brothers.

phrases: Thou shalt love the LORD thy God with all thine heart, **and** with all thy soul, **and** with all thy might.(Deuteronomy 6:5)

clauses: He must increase, **but** I must decrease. (John 3:30)

clauses: I will fear no evil: **for** thou art with me.

## Coordinating Conjunctions and Correlative Conjunctions

Both of the independent clauses in each of the above sentences contain a subject and a verb. Each clause expresses a complete thought and can stand by itself.

**Correlative conjunctions** come in pairs. They also connect words, phrases, or clauses of equal grammatical worth.

---
**Correlative Conjunctions**

either . . .or, neither . . . nor, not only . . .but also, both . . . and

---

Thou shalt **neither** vex a stranger, **nor** oppress him. (Exodus 22:21a)

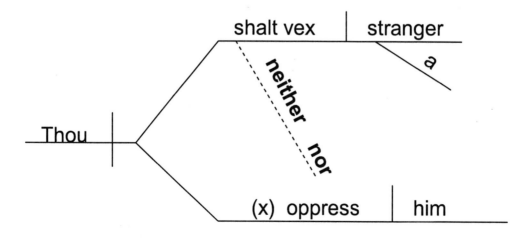

# Coordinating Conjunctions and Correlative Conjunctions

Study the examples. Each of the sentences has a compound element: compound independent clauses, compound predicates, compound prepositional phrases, compound direct objects. Each of these are connected by a **coordinating conjunction(s)** above a dotted line.

Directions for Practice Sheets

## Coordinating Conjunctions

1. Find the **coordinating conjunction** that connects words, phrases or clauses of equal rank.
2. Place it on top of a dotted line between the two equal parts.

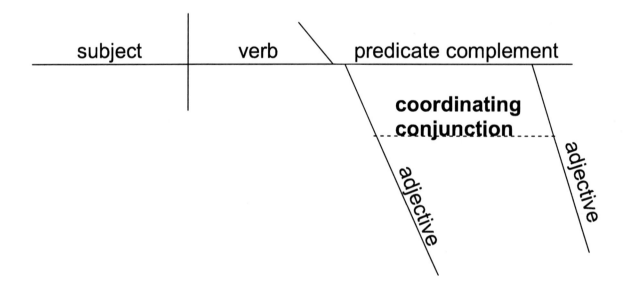

# Coordinating Conjunctions and Correlative Conjunctions
## Directions for Practice Sheets

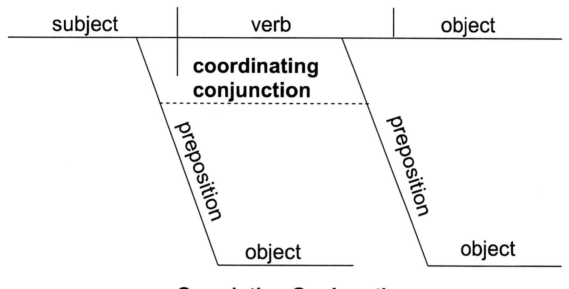

## Correlative Conjunctions

1. Find the **correlative conjunctions** that connect words, phrases or clauses of equal rank. They come in pairs.
2. Place them on top of a slanted dotted line between the two equal parts.

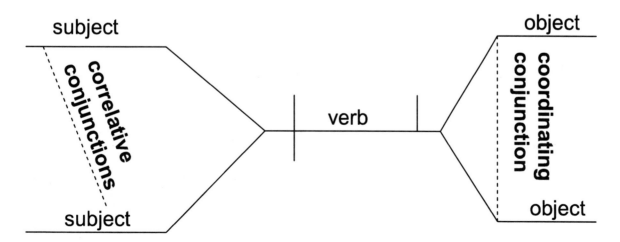

# Coordinating Conjunctions and Correlative Conjunctions
## Examples

1. He must increase, **but** I must decrease. (John 3:30)

```
      He  |  must increase
   ┌──────┼───────────────
but│
   │   I  |  must decrease
   └──────┼───────────────
```

2. I will never leave thee, **nor** forsake thee. (Hebrews 13:5c)

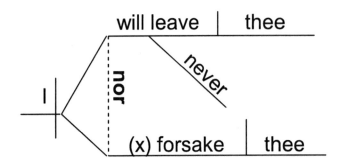

3. We are members of his body, of his flesh, **and** of his bones. (Ephesians 5:30)

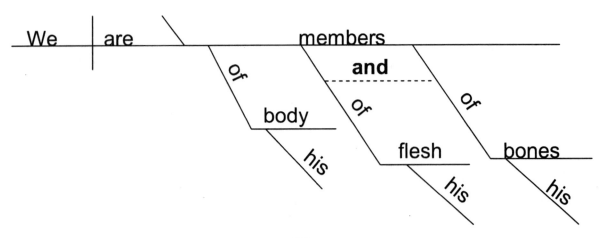

97

# Coordinating Conjunctions and Correlative Conjunctions

4. Love not the world, **neither** the things that are in the world. (1 John 2:15a)

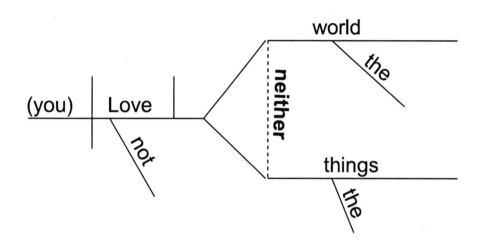

5. Thou shalt **neither** vex a stranger, **nor** oppress him. (Exodus 22:21a)

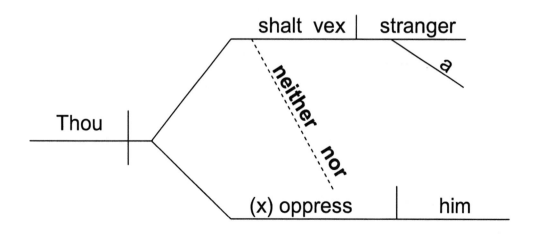

## Coordinating Conjunctions and Correlative Conjunctions
Practice Sheet

1. He will not always chide: **neither** will he keep his anger for ever. (Psalm 103:9)

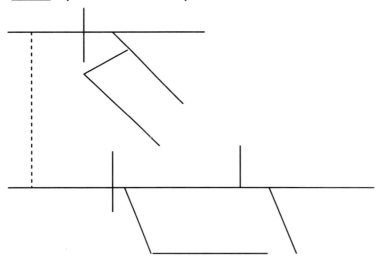

2. Behold, he that keepeth Israel shall **neither** slumber **nor** sleep. (Psalm 121:4)

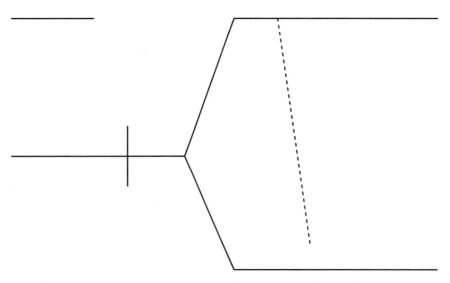

"That keepeth Israel" is not to be diagrammed. It will be taught in a later lesson.

# Coordinating Conjunctions and Correlative Conjunctions
## Practice Sheet

3. The LORD knoweth the way of the righteous: **but** the way of the ungodly shall perish. (Psalm 1:6)

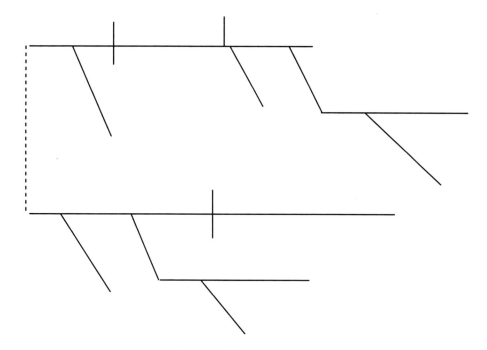

4. I will fear no evil: **for** thou art with me. (Psalm 23:4b)

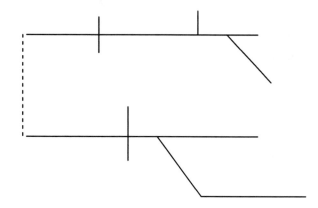

# Coordinating Conjunctions and Correlative Conjunctions
Practice Sheet

5. Thou shalt call his name JESUS:* **for** he shall save his people from their sins. (Matthew 1:21b)

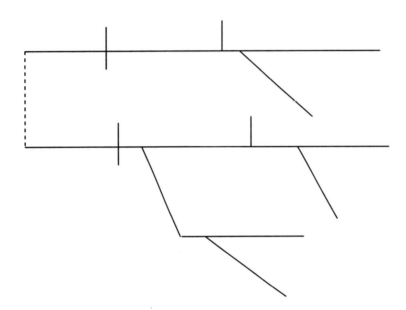

*The word "JESUS" is an objective complement. An **objective complement** is a noun, pronoun, or adjective which follows a direct object and renames it or tells what the direct object has become. The line between the direct object and the objective complement is slanted towards the direct object.

Example: John 13:13a

# Coordinating Conjunctions and Correlative Conjunctions
## Directions for Test

For each diagram with a **coordinating conjunction,** place the **coordinating conjunction** on a vertical dotted line between the words, phrases, or clauses of equal rank.

For each diagram with **correlative conjunctions,** place the **conjunctions** on a slanting vertical line between the words, phrases, or clauses of equal rank.

Example:

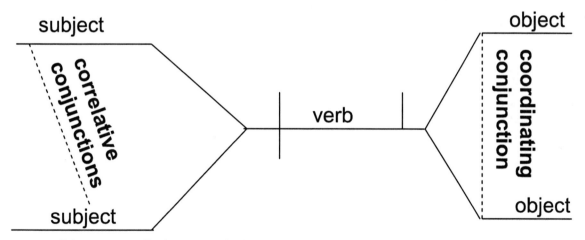

Diagram all the words in the sentences *except* those *not underlined* or in *dark print*. The underlined words have been in previous lessons, and the words in bold letters are the **conjunctions.** All the rest of the words will be studied in later lessons.

## Coordinating Conjunctions and Correlative Conjunctions
Test

1. They have ears, **but** they hear not. (Psalm 135:17a)

2. **Neither** fear ye their fear, **nor** be afraid. (Isaiah 8:12b)

3. I have **neither** lent on usury, **nor** men have lent to me on usury. (Jeremiah 15:10b)

4. I laid me down **and** slept; I awaked; **for** the LORD sustained me. (Psalm 3:5)

5. Heaven **and** earth shall pass away: **but** my words shall not pass away. (Luke 21:33)

## 21 - Diagramming Pronouns

**Pronouns** are words that take the place of nouns. Just as nouns, they can be subjects, direct objects, indirect objects, predicate complements, and objects of prepositions.

If the **pronoun** shows possession, it usually is used as an adjective. Possessive pronouns that can be adjectives are *my, your, our, his, her, its* and *their*. Review the different types of **pronouns** for usage (see page 12).

Directions: Study the examples.

1. The reflexive **pronoun** "**himself**" is used as an indirect object.
2. The reflexive **pronoun** "**himself**" is used as a direct object.

    The personal **pronoun "his"** indicates possession. It is used the same way that an adjective is used.

3. The interrogative **pronoun** "who" is used as a subject.
4. The indefinite **pronoun** "**None**" is used as a subject.

    The reflexive **pronouns** "**himself**" are used as objects of the preposition "to" and the personal **pronoun** "**us**" as object of the preposition "of" in both sentences 4 and 5.

5. The indefinite **pronoun** "**every one**" is used as a subject.

# Diagramming Pronouns
## Examples

1. <u>God</u> <u>will</u> <u>provide</u> **himself** <u>a</u> <u>lamb</u> <u>for</u> <u>a</u> <u>burnt</u> <u>offering</u>. (Genesis 22:8a)

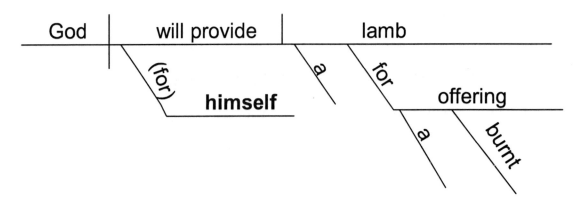

2. <u>David</u> <u>encouraged</u> **himself** <u>in</u> <u>the</u> <u>LORD</u> his God. (1 Samuel 30:6c)

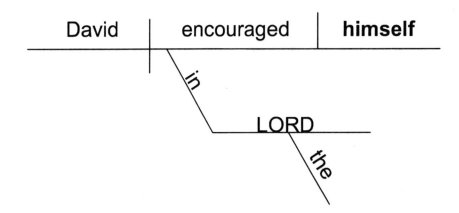

3. **Who** <u>can</u> <u>utter</u> <u>the</u> <u>mighty</u> <u>acts</u> <u>of</u> <u>the</u> <u>LORD</u>? (Psalm 106:2a)

# Diagramming Pronouns
## Examples

4. **None** of us liveth to **himself**, and no man dieth to **himself**. (Romans 14:7)

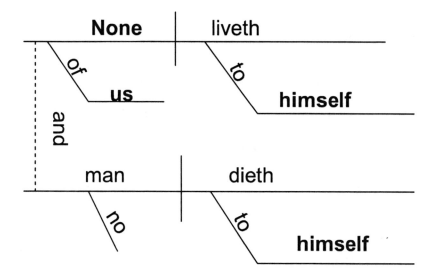

5. Then **every one** of us shall give account of **himself** to God. (Romans 14:12)

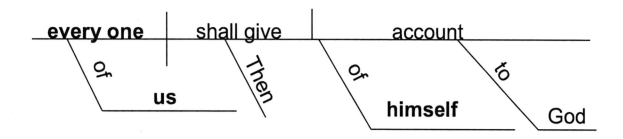

# Diagramming Pronouns
## Directions for Practice Pages

For each sentence do the following for **pronouns**:

1. Find a word that could take the place of a noun.
2. Determine if the **pronoun** is used as a noun in the sentence: subject, indirect object, direct object, predicate complement, or object of the preposition.
3. Place it in the appropriate part of the diagram.
4. Determine if the **pronoun** is used as an adjective.
5. Place it on the slanted line under the noun that it modifies.

Examples:

Here am I; send me. (Isaiah 6:8c)

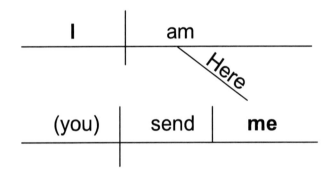

Thou art the God of my salvation. (Psalm 25:5b)

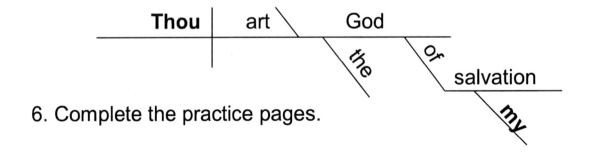

6. Complete the practice pages.

# Diagramming Pronouns
## Practice Sheet

1. The LORD revealed **himself** to Samuel in Shiloh by the word of the LORD. (1 Samuel 3:21)

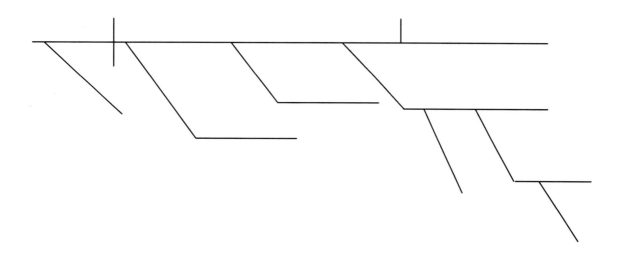

2. **I** thought on **my** ways, and turned **my** feet unto **thy** testimonies. (Psalm 119:59)

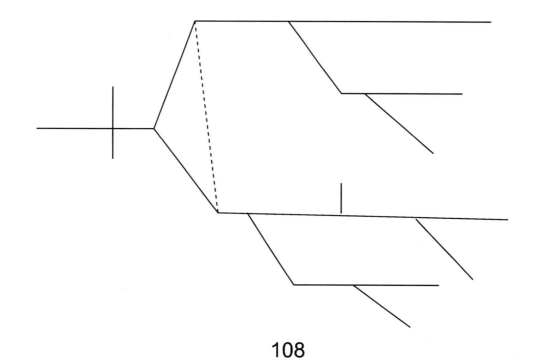

# Diagramming Pronouns
## Practice Sheet

3. <u>For</u> **thy** <u>name's</u> <u>sake</u>, <u>O LORD</u>, <u>pardon</u> **mine** <u>iniquity</u>; <u>for</u> **it** <u>is</u> <u>great</u>. (Psalm 25:11)

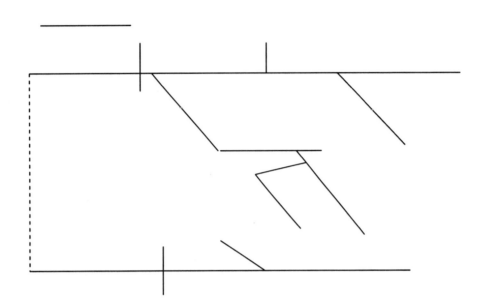

4. **He** [the Lord] <u>brought</u> **them** <u>out of</u> <u>darkness</u> <u>and</u> <u>the</u> <u>shadow</u> <u>of</u> <u>death</u>. (Psalm 107:14a)

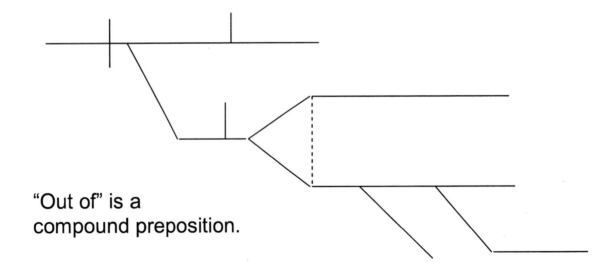

"Out of" is a compound preposition.

109

# Diagramming Pronouns
## Practice Sheet

5. Nevertheless I am continually with thee: **thou** <u>hast holden</u> **me** <u>by</u> **my** <u>right hand</u>. (Psalm 73:23b)

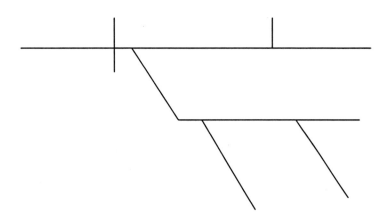

# Diagramming Pronouns
## Directions for Test

Diagram the test sentences. Remember that **possessive pronouns** are used as adjectives. They are **pronouns** because they refer to noun or **pronoun** antecedents. However, they have the character of adjectives because they modify nouns or pronouns.

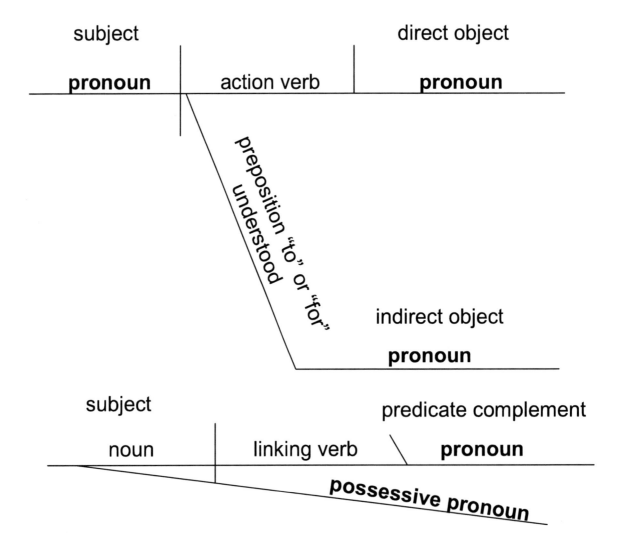

## Diagramming Pronouns
Test

1. [**you**, the LORD] O visit **me** with **thy** salvation. (Psalm 106:4b)

2. **We** have sinned with **our** fathers. (Psalm 106:6a)

3. **He** [the LORD] led **them** forth by the right way. (Psalm 107:7a)

4, **She** [a virtuous woman] will do **him** good and not evil all the days of **her** life. (Proverbs 31:12)

5. The ants are a people not strong, yet **they** prepare **their** meat in the summer. (Proverbs 30:25)

## 22 - Diagramming Infinitives

Like participles, **infinitives** are verbals, too. In form, they are verbs, but in usage they may be nouns, adjectives, or adverbs. They usually begin with the word "to" followed by a verb.

Study these examples: **Infinitive used as a noun - subject**

**To obey** is better than **sacrifice.** (1 Samuel 15:22b)

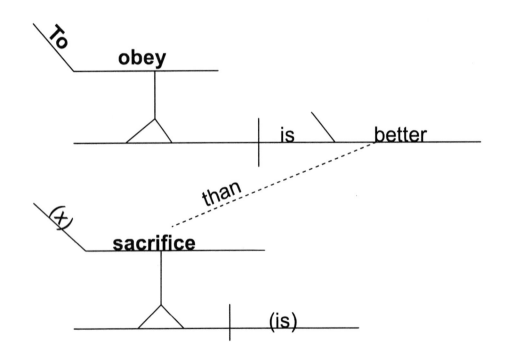

# Diagramming Infinitives

## Infinitive Phrase ("clause") with Its Own Subject Used as a Direct Object

<u>Let</u> **brotherly love continue.** (Hebrews 13:1)

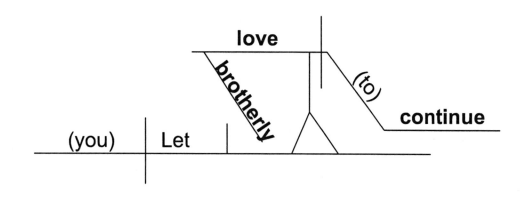

This **infinitive phrase** has its own subject (love) and a verb form. This gives the character of a clause. If the subject of the **infinitive** is a pronoun, it must be in the objective form, not the usual subjective form.

# Diagramming Infinitives

## Infinitive used as an adverb

<u>Young</u> <u>men</u> <u>likewise</u> <u>exhort</u> **to be sober minded**.

(Titus 2:6)

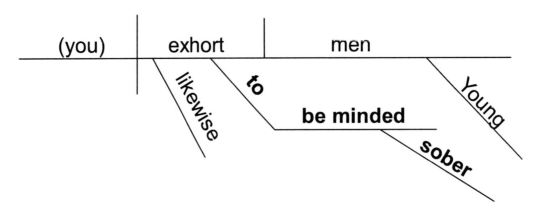

Notice how the **infinitives** used as nouns are placed on a horizontal subject-verb line which is placed on a forked line above the main subject-verb line. The adjectives and adverbs are placed diagonally on a structure similar to one made for prepositional phrases below the word(s) they modify.

Study the examples. In all of these sentences, the **infinitive phrases** are direct objects. The whole **infinitive phrase** ("clause") is printed in dark print.

Remember that "to" plus a noun or pronoun is a prepositional phrase. "To" plus a verb is an **infinitive phrase.**

# Diagramming Infinitives
## Examples

1. <u>Let</u> **thy tender mercies come unto me,** that I may live. (Psalm 119:77a)

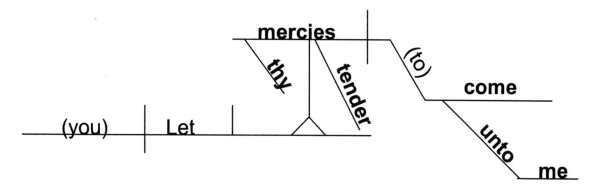

2. <u>Let</u> **my heart be sound in thy statutes**; that I be not ashamed. (Psalm 119:80)

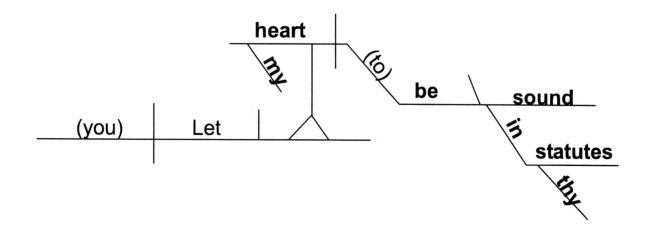

# Diagramming Infinitives
## Examples

3. <u>Make</u> **thy face to shine upon thy servant;** <u>and</u> <u>teach</u> <u>me</u> <u>thy statutes</u>. (Psalm 119:135)

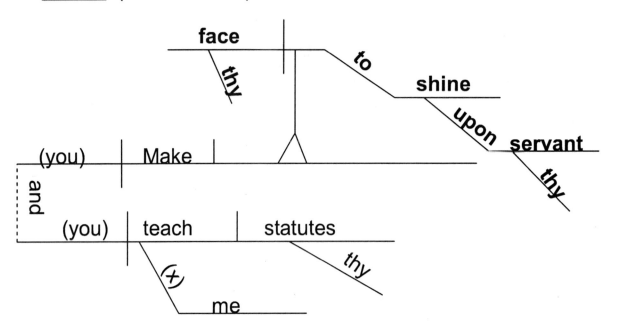

4. <u>Let</u> **thine hand help me**; <u>for</u> <u>I</u> <u>have chosen</u> <u>thy</u> <u>precepts</u>. (Psalm 119:173)

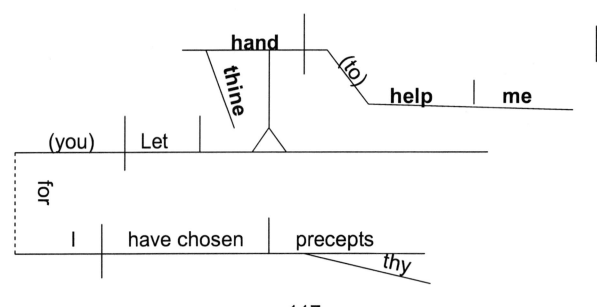

## Diagramming Infinitives
Examples

5. He causeth his wind to blow, and the waters flow.
(Psalm 147:18b)

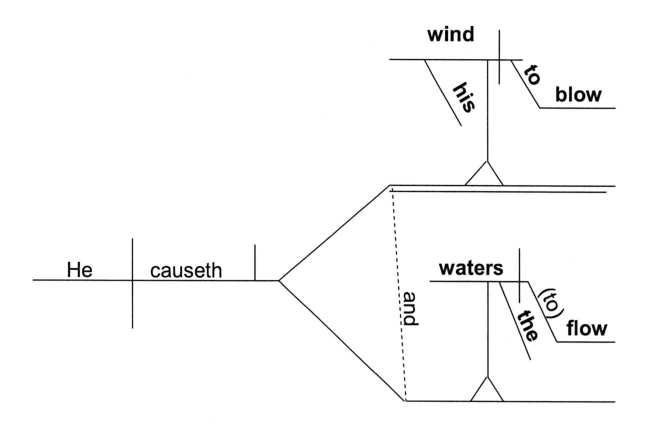

# Diagramming Infinitives
## Directions for Practice Sheets

For each sentence, do the following:

1. Locate the **infinitive**.

2. Decide whether the **infinitive** is used as a subject, direct object, predicate complement, adjective or adverb.

3. Place the **infinitives** or **infinitive phrases** used as nouns on the horizontal subject-verb line which is placed on a forked line above the main subject-verb line.

4. Place the **infinitives** or **infinitive phrases** used as adjectives or adverbs on the structure similar to that used for prepositional phrases below what they modify. The word "to" is placed on the slanted line, and the verb is placed on the horizontal line. Modifiers of the infinitive are placed on slanted lines beneath the verb.

5. Complete the practice sheets.

Diagram all the words in the sentences *except* those *not underlined* or in *dark print*.

# Diagramming Infinitives
## Practice Sheet

1. The fear of the LORD is **to hate evil.** (Proverbs 8:13a)

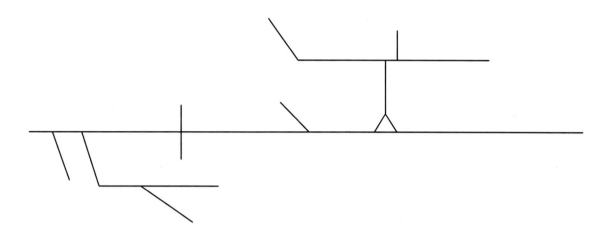

2. He (the Spirit of the LORD) hath sent **me to heal the brokenhearted**. (The subject of the infinitive is always in the objective case. "Me" is the object pronoun form.)

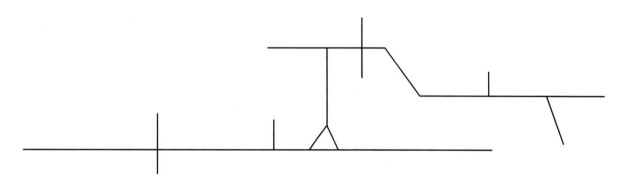

3. Lo, I come **to do thy will**, O God. (Hebrews 10:9a)

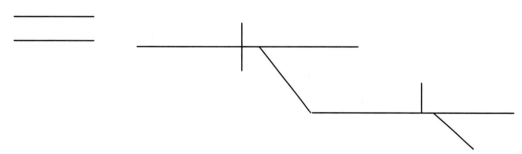

# Diagramming Infinitives
## Practice Sheet

4. Let **her own works praise her in the gates**.
(Proverbs 31:31b)

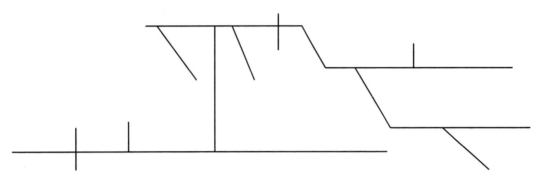

5. The wisdom of the prudent is **to understand his way**.
(Proverbs 14:8a)

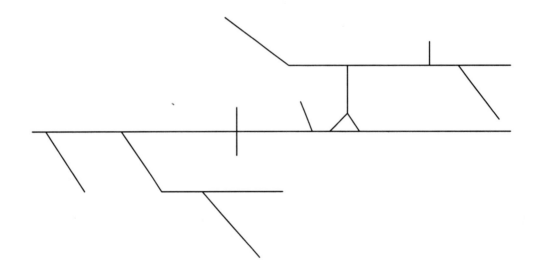

## Diagramming Infinitives
Directions for Test

For each sentence do the following:

1. Locate the **infinitive**.

2. Decide whether it is used as a subject, direct object, predicate complement, adjective or adverb.

3. Place **infinitives** or **infinitive phrases** used as nouns on a horizontal subject-verb line which is placed on a forked line above the main subject-verb line.

4. Slant the **infinitives** or **infinitive phrases** used as adjectives or adverbs on a structure similar to that used for prepositional phrases below what they modify.

5. Diagram all the test sentences.

## Diagramming Infinitives
Test

1. **To do good** <u>and</u> **to communicate** <u>forget</u> <u>not</u>.

    (Hebrews 13:16a)

2. <u>The</u> <u>LORD</u> <u>make</u> **you to increase** <u>and</u> **abound in love**.

    (1 Thessalonians 3:12a)

3. <u>Let</u> **no man despise thy youth**. (1 Timothy 4:12a)

4. <u>Go</u> <u>not</u> <u>forth</u> <u>hastily</u> **to strive**. (Proverbs 25:8a)

5. <u>Let</u> **us consider one another to provoke unto love** <u>and</u> **to good works**. (Hebrews 10:24)

## 23 - Diagramming Gerunds

A **gerund** is a verbal noun. It is a verb in form and a noun in usage. It is a verb because it ends in "ing", "ed" or "en." It is a noun because it is used as a subject, an object, a predicate complement or an appositive. (Appositives will be studied later.)

Directions: Study the examples.

1. "**Understanding**" is a **gerund**. It ends in "ing" and is an object of the verb "give." "According to" is a two-word preposition.

2. "**Broken**" is a **gerund**. It ends in "en" and is used as an object of the verb "healeth."

3. "**Downsitting**" and "**uprising**" end in "ing" and are used as objects of the verb "knowest."

4. "**Trembling**" ends in "ing" and is used as an object of the preposition "with."

5. "**Doing**" ends in "ing" and is used as a predicate complement. It means the same as "This."

## Diagramming Gerunds

**Gerunds** like other nouns may have modifiers such as adjectives or prepositional phrases. These modifiers are placed beneath the **gerunds** just as they would be for any other nouns.

Directions for Practice Sheets

For each diagram, do the following for **gerunds:**

1. Find the **gerund,** a word that usually ends in *ing, ed,* or *en* that is used as a noun. Nouns can be used as *subjects, direct objects, predicate complements, indirect objects,* or *objects of prepositions.*

2. Place the slanted **gerund** on the "staircase" above the subject-verb line or above the horizontal line for the object of the preposition.

3. Place any modifiers beneath it like direct adjectives or prepositional phrases.

Diagram all the words in the sentences *except* those *not underlined* or in *dark print*. The underlined words have been in previous lessons, and the words in bold letters are the **gerunds**. All the rest of the words will be studied in later lessons.

# Diagramming Gerunds
## Examples

1. Give me **understanding** according to thy word. (Psalm 119:169b)

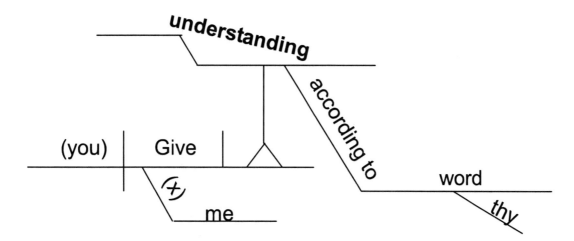

2. He healeth the **broken** in heart, and bindeth up their wounds. (Psalm 147:3)

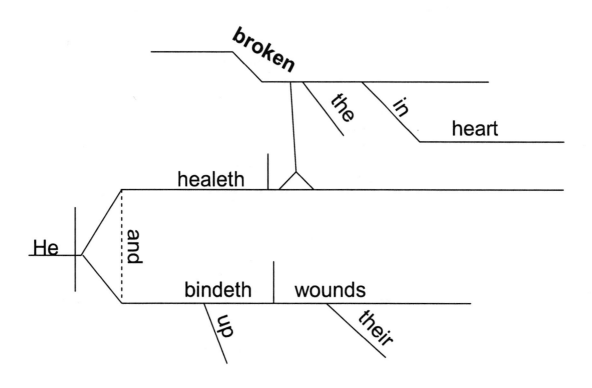

# Diagramming Gerunds
Examples

3. Thou knowest my downsitting and mine uprising.
(Psalm 139:2a)

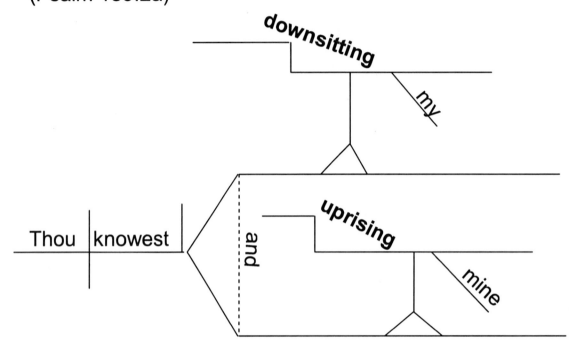

4. Serve the LORD with fear, and rejoice with trembling.
(Psalm 2:11)

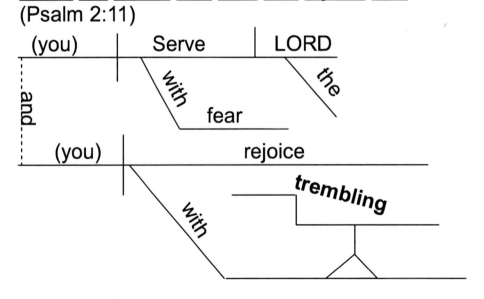

# Diagramming Gerunds
## Examples

5. This is the LORD's **doing**; it is marvellous in our eyes. (Psalm 118:23)

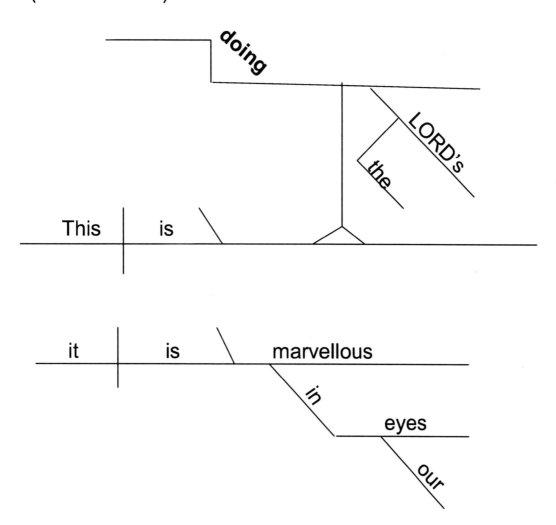

# Diagramming Gerunds
## Practice Sheet

1. Remove from me the way of **lying**. (Psalm 119:29a)

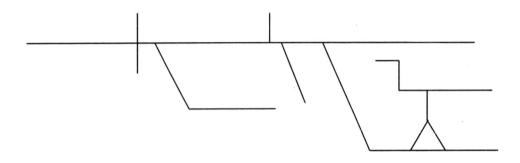

2. Give me **understanding**, and I shall keep thy law. (Psalm 119:34a)

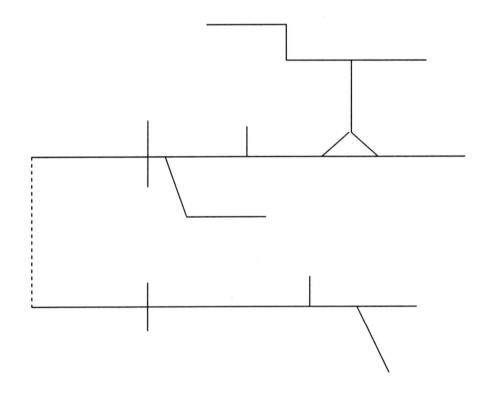

## Diagramming Gerunds
Practice Sheet

3. I hate and abhor **lying**: but thy law do I love. (Psalm 119:163)

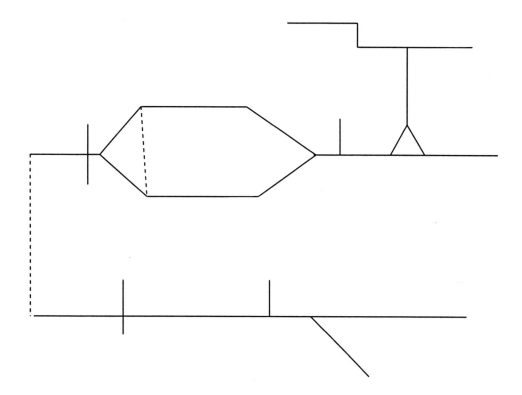

4. **Blessings** are upon the head of the just. (Proverbs 10:6a)

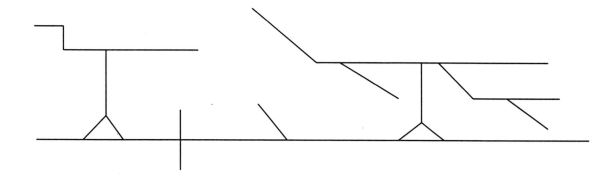

# Diagramming Gerunds
## Practice Sheet

5. Good **understanding** giveth favour. (Proverbs 13:15a)

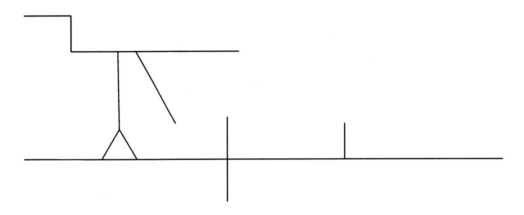

# Diagramming Gerunds
## Directions for Test

For each diagram, do the following for **gerunds**:

1. Find a **gerund**, a word that ends in *ing, ed* or *en* and is used as a noun.

2. Wherever the **gerund** goes, slant it above a "staircase" that is placed on a forked line joined to the subject-verb line. If the **gerund** is an object, slant it above a "staircase" on the horizontal line wherever the indirect object, a direct object or an object of a preposition goes.

3. Place any direct adjective or modifying prepositional phrase beneath the **gerund**.

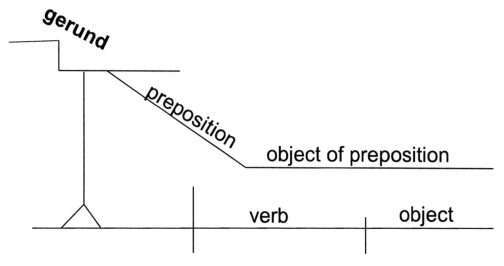

Diagram all the words in the sentences *except* those *not underlined* or in *dark print*. The underlined words have been in previous lessons, and the words in bold letters are the **gerunds**. All the rest of the words will be studied in later lessons.

## Diagramming Gerunds
Test

1. My son, God will provide himself a lamb for a burnt **offering**. (Genesis 22:8a) (Do not diagram the words, "My son.")

2. Turn away mine eyes from **beholding** vanity. (Psalm 119:37a)

3. Without **shedding** of blood is no remission. (Hebrews 9:22b)

4. The righteous eateth to the **satisfying** of his soul. (Proverbs 13:25a)

5. Even a child is known by his **doings**. (Proverbs 20:11a)

## 24 - Diagramming Appositives

An **appositive** is a noun or pronoun that usually follows another noun or pronoun and renames it. A comma may separate the appositive from the word it renames.

Examples:

Trust ye in the LORD for ever: for in the LORD **JEHOVAH** is everlasting strength. (Isaiah 26:4)

The noun **JEHOVAH** follows the noun *LORD* and means the same person.

The Father **himself** loveth you. (John 16:27a)

The pronoun **himself** follows the noun *Father* and means the same person.

Sometimes an **appositive** has modifiers and is part of a phrase.

Blessed be the LORD, **my strength.** (Psalm 144:1a)

The appositive **strength** is modified by the adjective *my*. The two words form an **appositive phrase**.

## Diagramming Appositives

**The blessing of the LORD**, it maketh rich, and he addeth no sorrow with it. (Proverbs 10:22)

The **appositive** *blessing* has the adjective *the* and the prepositional phrase *of the LORD* modifying it. This **appositive phrase** precedes the pronoun it renames.

The tongue is a fire, **a world of iniquity**. (James 3:6a)

The **appositive** *world* has the adjective *a* and the prepositional phrase *of iniquity* modifying it. All of these words make up an **appositive phrase**.

Directions for Practice Sheet

For each diagram, do the following for **appositives**:

1. Find the **appositive,** a word that renames nouns or pronouns.
2. Place it next to the word that it renames.
3. Put parentheses around it.
4. Place the direct adjective(s) on slanted lines beneath the appositive.
5. Place any other modifiers such as prepositional phrases beneath the appositive.

Fill in the diagrams on the practice sheets.

# Diagramming Appositives
## Examples

1. Blessed be the LORD, **my strength.** (Psalm 144:1a)

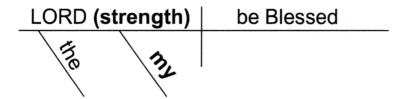

2. Trust ye in the LORD for ever: for in the LORD **JEHOVAH** is everlasting strength. (Isaiah 26:4)

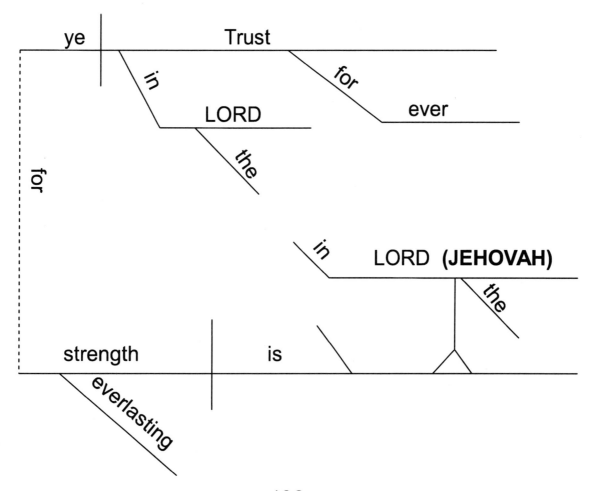

## Diagramming Appositives

3. **The blessing of the LORD**, it maketh rich, and he addeth no sorrow with it. (Proverbs 10:22)

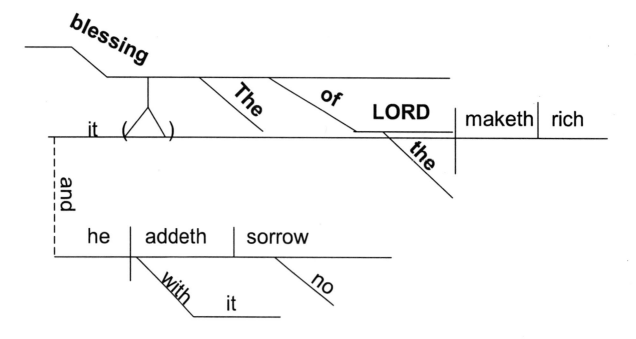

4. The tongue is a fire, **a world of iniquity**. (James 3:6a)

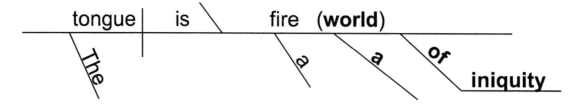

5. The Father **himself** loveth you. (John 16:27a)

# Diagramming Appositives
## Practice Sheet

1. I **Jesus** have sent mine angel to testify unto you these things in the churches. (Revelation 22:16a)

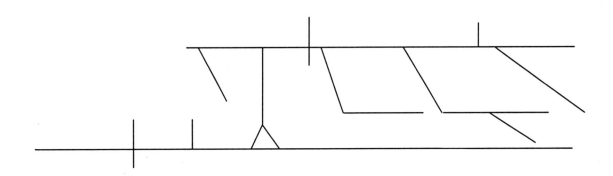

2. I **the LORD** will hear them. (Isaiah 41:17c)

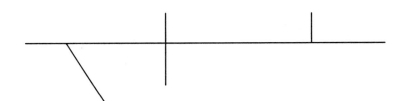

3. Alexander **the coppersmith** did me much evil. (2 Timothy 4:14a)

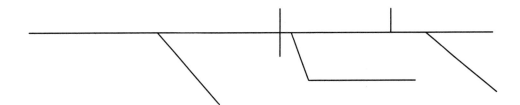

## Diagramming Appositives
Practice Sheet

4. The word of the LORD came expressly unto Ezekiel **the priest.** (Ezekiel 1:3a)

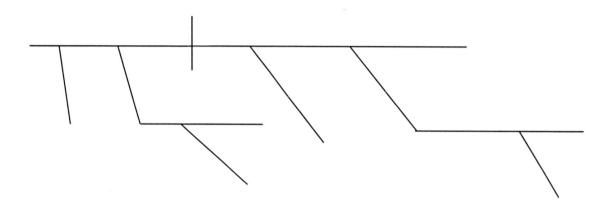

5. Thou art the Christ, **the Son of the living God**. (Matthew 16:16b)

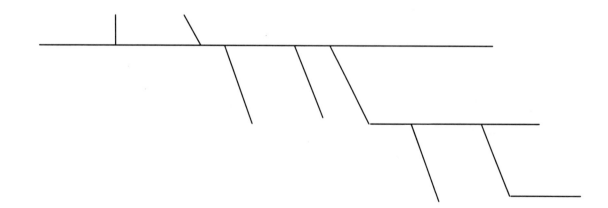

# Diagramming Appositives
## Directions for Test

For each diagram do the following for **appositives:**

1. Find a noun or pronoun that renames another noun or pronoun and is not a predicate complement.
2. Put parentheses around it and place it next to the word that it renames on the horizontal line.
3. Put any modifiers of the **appositive**, words or phrases, underneath it.

Example:

The tongue is a fire, **a world of iniquity**. (James 3:6a)

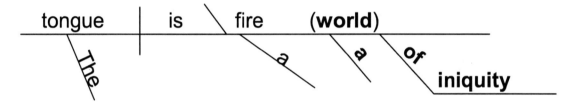

The word *fire* renames the word *tongue* but comes after a linking verb. Such a word is a predicate complement.

The word *world* is an appositive because it renames *fire* and does not come after a linking verb.

Diagram all the words in the sentences *except* those *not underlined* or in *dark print*. The underlined words have been in previous lessons and the words in bold letters are the **appositives.** All the rest of the words will be studied later.

## Diagramming Appositives
Test

1. God is our refuge and strength, **a very present help in trouble**. (Psalm 46:1)

2. The LORD also will be a refuge for the oppressed, **a refuge in times of trouble**. (Psalm 9:9)

3. The LORD is good, **a strong hold in the day of trouble**. (Nahum 1:7a)

4. Salute Urbane, **our helper in Christ**. (Romans 16:9a)

5. Be not thou therefore ashamed of the testimony of our Lord, nor of me **his prisoner**. (2 Timothy 1:8a)

## 25 - Diagramming Nouns of Address

A **noun of address** is a noun that names the person addressed. Some **nouns of address** have no modifiers; they are used alone to address a person.

Examples:

O **LORD**, thou hast searched me, and known me.

(Psalm 139:1)

**LORD**, who shall abide in thy tabernacle?

(Psalm 15:1a)

Ye, **brethren**, be not weary in well doing.

(2 Thessalonians 3:13)

Some **nouns of address** do have adjectives that modify them.

Examples:

**My son**, despise not the chastening of the LORD.

(Proverbs 3:11a)

Do not err, **my beloved brethren**. (James 1:16)

# Diagramming Nouns of Address

Study the examples. Note that the **noun of direct address** is placed on a horizontal line above the sentence, and all modifiers are placed on slanted lines beneath it.

## Directions for Practice Sheets

For each sentence do the following:
1. Find the noun that addresses a person or a group of persons.
2. Place it on a horizontal line above and on the left of the subject-verb line.

Example:

O **Israel**, trust thou in the Lord. (Psalm 115:9a)

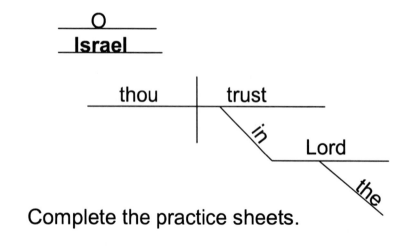

Complete the practice sheets.

# Diagramming Nouns of Address
## Examples

1. O **LORD**, thou hast searched me, and known me. (Psalm 139:1)

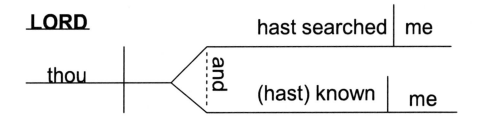

2. **My son**, despise not the chastening of the LORD. (Proverbs 3:11a)

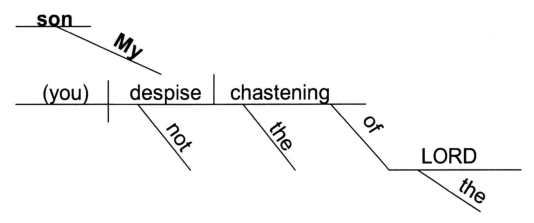

3. **LORD**, who shall abide in thy tabernacle? (Psalm 15:1a)

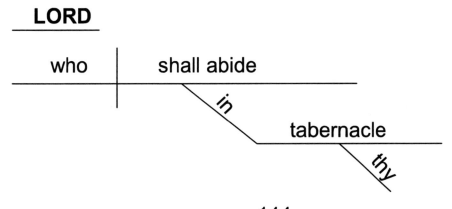

# Diagramming Nouns of Address
## Examples

4. Ye, **brethren**, be not weary in well doing.
   (2 Thessalonians 3:13)

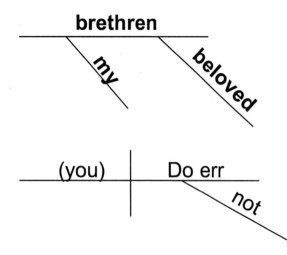

5. Do not err, **my beloved brethren**. (James 1:16)

# Diagramming Nouns of Address
## Practice Sheet

1. **Little children**, keep yourselves from idols. Amen. (1 John 5:21)

2. Who art thou, **LORD**? (Acts 9:5a)

3. Lo, I come to do thy will, O **God**. (Hebrews 10:9a)

# Diagramming Nouns of Address
Practice Sheet

4. **LORD**, evermore give us this bread. (John 6:34b)

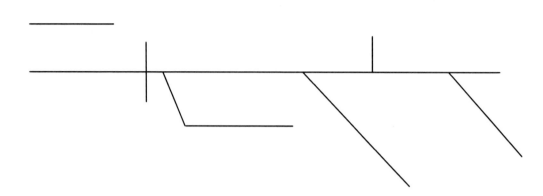

5. **My son**, God will provide himself a lamb for a burnt offering. (Genesis 22:8a)

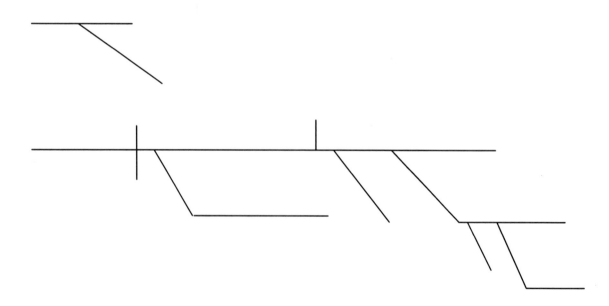

## Diagramming Nouns of Address
Directions for Test

For each sentence, do the following:

1. Find the noun that addresses a person or a group of persons.
2. Place it on a horizontal line above and on the left of the subject-verb line.
3. If the noun has a modifier, put a slanted line underneath the noun and place the modifier on top of the slanted line.

Example:

**Our Father** which art in heaven, <u>Hallowed</u> <u>be</u> <u>thy</u> <u>name</u>. (Matthew 6:9b)

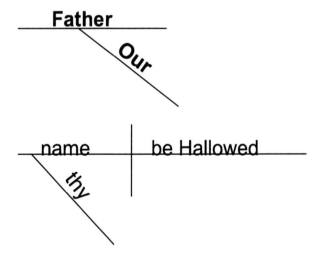

Remember the underlined words have been in previous lessons, and the words in bold letters are the **nouns of address**. All the rest of the words will be studied in later lessons.

Diagram the test sentences.

**Diagramming Nouns of Address**
Test

1. Now, **little children**, abide in him. (1 John 2:28a)

2. Why are ye fearful, O **ye of little faith**? (Matthew 8:26a)

3. **Son of man**, can these bones live? (Ezekiel 37:3a)

4. **LORD**, teach us to pray. (Luke 11:1c)

5. Bless the LORD, O **my soul**. (Psalm 103:1a)

## 26 - Unit 2 Test

Directions: Diagram the following sentences.

1. I waited patiently for the LORD; and he inclined unto me, and heard my cry. (Psalm 40:1)

2. The statutes of the LORD are right, rejoicing the heart. (Psalm 19:8a)

3. Many, O LORD my God, are thy wonderful works. (Psalm 40:5a)

4. Be pleased, O LORD, to deliver me. (Psalm 40:13a)

5. The fear of the LORD is the beginning of wisdom. (Psalm 111:10a)

# Unit 3

## Diagramming Clauses

27. Diagramming Noun Clauses ............................ 152

28. Diagramming Adjective Clauses ..................... 164

29. Diagramming Adverbial Clauses ..................... 173

30. Unit 3 - Test ..................................................... 184

## 27 - Diagramming Noun Clauses

A clause is a group of words that has a subject and a verb. Some clauses are independent. They can stand by themselves. Some are dependent; they begin with a word that connects them to an independent clause. They cannot stand by themselves.

A **noun clause** is a dependent clause and is used wherever a noun can be used: subject, indirect object, direct object, predicate complement, object of preposition, and appositive.

**Noun clauses** are introduced by signal words. These words may come at the beginning of **noun clauses**.

| **Signal Words** | | | | |
|---|---|---|---|---|
| how | whatever | which | whomever | whether |
| if | when | who | whose | whoever |
| that | where | whom | what | why |

Directions: Study the examples.

1. The **noun clause** is used as a direct object. "That thy judgments are right" answers the question "What?" after the question "I know what?"

2. The **noun clause** is used as a subject. It answers the question "Who?" before the predicate "is a wise son."

## Diagramming Noun Clauses

3. The **noun clause** in the third sentence is used as an appositive. It renames the pronoun *he*.
4. The **noun clause** in the fourth sentence is used as a subject. It answers the question "Who shall have mercy?"
5. The **noun clause** in the fifth sentence is used as a subject. It answers the question "Who findeth a good thing and obtaineth favour of the LORD?"

# Diagramming Noun Clauses
## Examples

1. <u>I</u> <u>know</u>, <u>O</u> <u>LORD</u>, **that thy judgments are right**. (Psalm 119:75a)

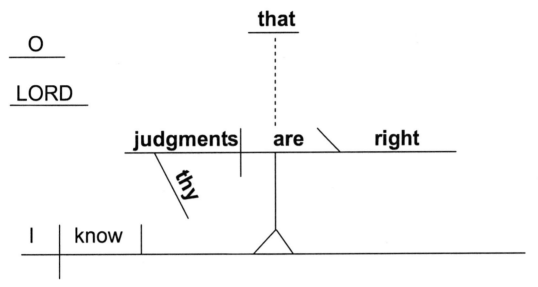

2. **Whoso keepeth the law** <u>is</u> <u>a</u> <u>wise</u> <u>son</u>. (Proverbs 28:7a)

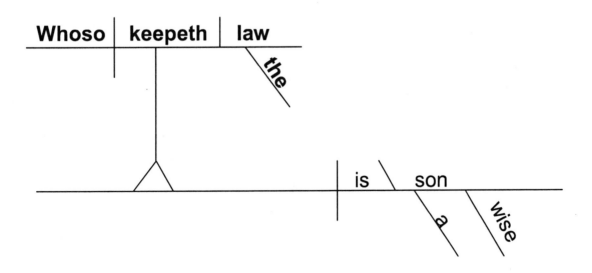

## Diagramming Noun Clauses
## Examples

3. **Whoso trusteth in the LORD**, happy is he.
   (Proverbs 16:20b)

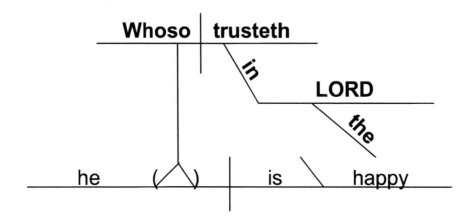

4. **Whoso confesseth and forsaketh them** [sins] shall have mercy. (Proverbs 28:13b)

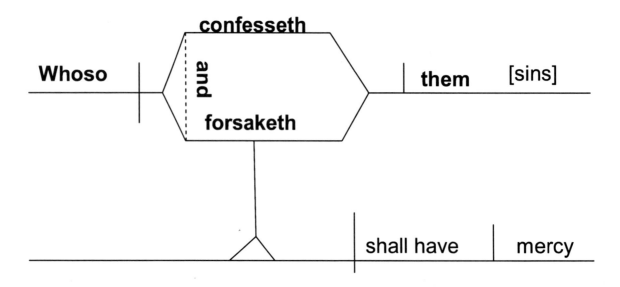

## Diagramming Noun Clauses
### Examples

5. **Whoso findeth a wife** <u>findeth a good thing, and obtaineth favour of the LORD</u>. (Proverbs 18:22)

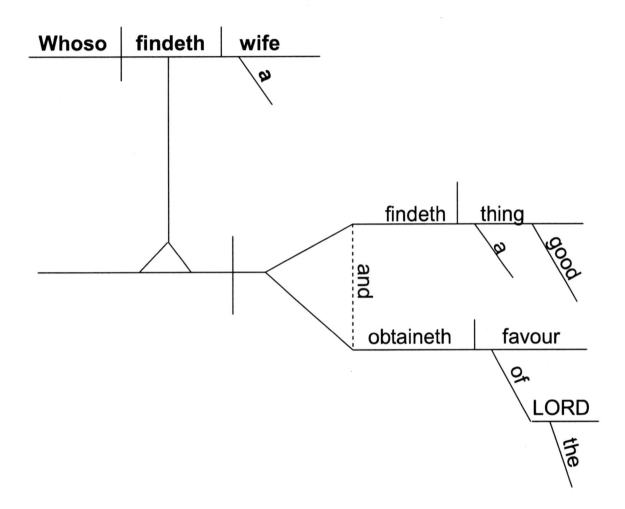

## Diagramming Noun Clauses
Directions for Practice Sheets

Do the following for each sentence:

1. Find the dependent clause used as a noun.

2. Put the subject of the noun clause on the base line above the forked lines or "stilt," then the verb after the vertical line, then the direct object or predicate complement after the direct-object or predicate-complement line.

3. Put the rest of the sentence back down on the base line below.

# Diagramming Noun Clauses
## Practice Sheet

1. **Whoso putteth his trust in the LORD** <u>shall</u> <u>be</u> <u>safe</u>.
   (Proverbs 29:25b)

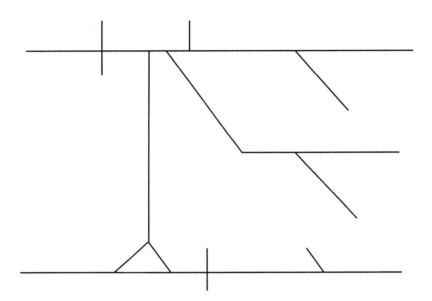

2. **Whosoever shall call upon the name of the LORD** <u>shall</u> <u>be</u> <u>saved</u>. (Romans 10:13)

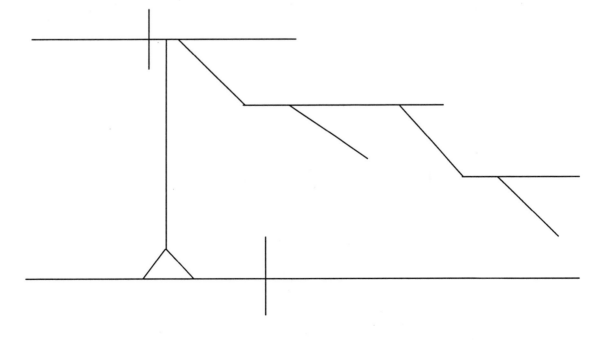

# Diagramming Noun Clauses
Practice Sheet

3. <u>This</u> <u>is</u> <u>love</u>, **that we walk after his commandments.** (2 John 1:6a)

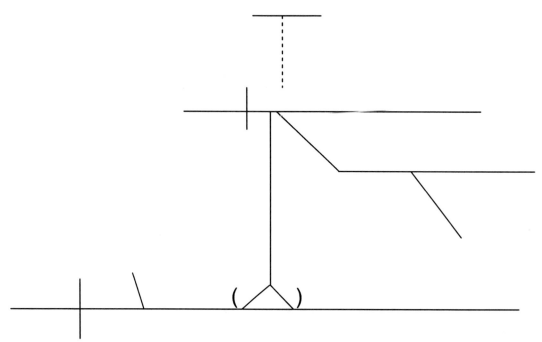

4. <u>Be</u> <u>still</u>, <u>and</u> <u>know</u> **that I am God.** (Psalm 46:10a)

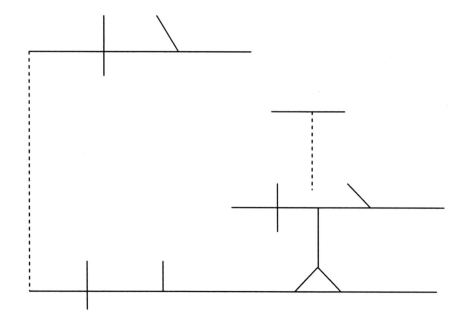

## Diagramming Noun Clauses
### Practice Sheet

5. **Whosoever denieth the Son**, the same hath not the Father.
   (1 John 2:23a)

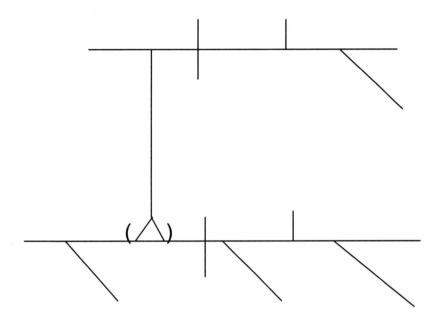

# Diagramming Noun Clauses
## Directions for Test

For each sentence do the following:

1. Find the **noun clause**.
2. Decide whether the **noun clause** is used as a subject, direct object, indirect object, predicate complement, appositive, or an object of a preposition.
3. If it is used as a subject, place it on a horizontal line above a forked line attached to the base line before the main verb.
4. If it is used as one of the other noun functions, place it on a horizontal line above a forked line attached to the base line wherever that noun function belongs.

Example:

**Noun Clause** used as an Appositive to a Subject

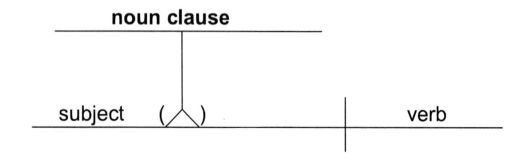

## Diagramming Noun Clauses
Directions for Test

5. If a **noun clause** is introduced with the word "that," place the word "that" on a horizontal line on a standard above the **noun clause.**

Example:

**Noun Clause** used as a Direct Object with Signal Word "That"

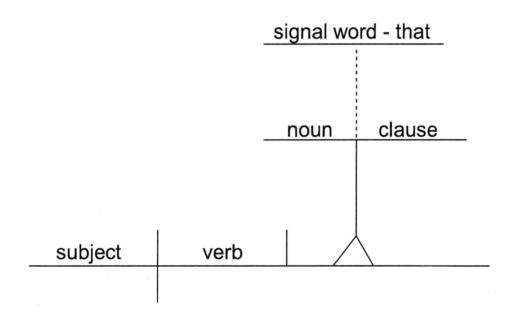

## Diagramming Noun Clauses
### Test

1. See **that ye love one another with a pure heart fervently**.

    (1 Peter 1:22b)

2. It doth not yet appear **what we shall be**. (1 John 3:2b)

3. **Whosoever believeth that Jesus is the Christ** is born of

    God. (1 John 5:1a)

4. I know **that the LORD is great**. (Psalm 135:5a)

5. The fire shall try every man's work of **what sort it is**.

    (1 Corinthians 3:13c)

## 28 - Diagramming Adjective Clauses

An **adjective clause** is a group of words with a subject and a verb. The whole clause is used as an adjective to modify a noun or a pronoun. The clause has a relative pronoun or adjective that links it to the independent clause.

---

### Relative Pronouns

**who, whom, which, that, whichever, whoever, whomever, whatever, whichsoever\*, whosoever\*, whomsoever\*, whatsoever\***

\*These words are rarely used in modern English.

### Relative Adjective

**whose**

---

Directions:

Study the examples. The **adjective clause** is put in dark print. Look for the relative pronoun or adjective that introduces the **adjective clause**. Read the explanation for each sentence.

## Diagramming Adjective Clauses

Examples:

1. The pronoun "he" is modified by the **adjective clause "that believeth on the Son."** The relative pronoun "that" links the **adjective clause** to the independent clause.

2. The pronoun "he" is modified by the **adjective clause "that believeth not the Son."** The relative pronoun "that" links the **adjective clause** to the independent clause.

3. The pronoun "he" is modified by the **adjective clause "that walketh uprightly."** The relative pronoun "that" links the **adjective clause** to the independent clause.

4. The pronoun "he" is modified by the **adjective clause "that is a companion of riotous men."** The relative pronoun "that" links the **adjective clause** to the independent clause.

5. The pronoun "him" is modified by the **adjective clause "that hath understanding."** The word "that" links the **adjective clause** to the independent clause.

# Diagramming Adjective Clauses
## Examples

1. He that believeth on the Son hath everlasting life.   (John 3:36a)

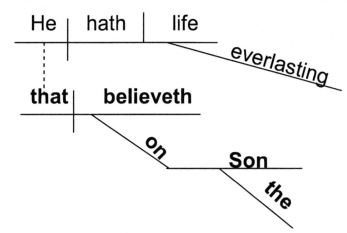

2. He that believeth not the Son shall not see life. (John 3:36b)

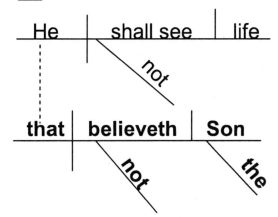

3. He that walketh uprightly walketh surely. (Proverbs 10:9a)

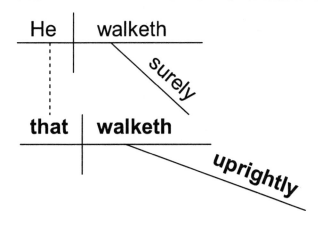

# Diagramming Adjective Clauses
## Examples

4. He that is a companion of riotous men shameth his father. (Proverbs 28:7b)

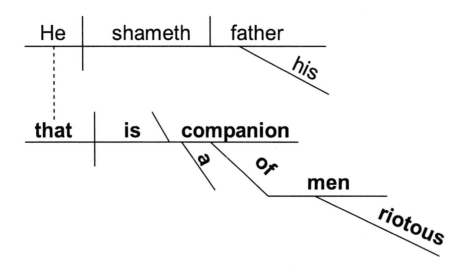

5. In the lips of him that hath understanding wisdom is found. (Proverbs 10:13a)

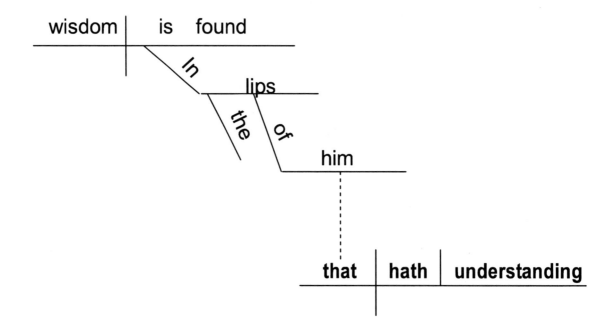

## Diagramming Adjective Clauses
Directions for Practice Sheets

Study the practice sheets before you fill in the diagrams.

The first four sentences are similar to the examples. The fifth sentence contains an **adjective clause** and a noun clause. Find the clauses and ask "What question does this clause answer?" Does it answer "What?" or "Who?" *before* the verb? If it does, then it is used as a subject. Does it answer "What?" or "Who?" *after* the verb? If it does, it is a direct object. Does it answer the question "Which one?" or "Whose?" If it does, then it is an adjective. **Adjective clauses** answer the same questions that single-word adjectives do.

Sentence 2 on the practice sheet contains a *nominal.* Nominals function as nouns but are not nouns themselves. Prepositions sometimes perform this function when they are used in conjunction with the verb *to be.* For example:

Every one **that is *of the truth*** heareth my voice.

(John 18:37c)

See page 191 for further explanation of *nominals*.

# Diagramming Adjective Clauses
## Practice Sheet

1. They **that sow in tears** shall reap in joy. (Psalm 126:5)

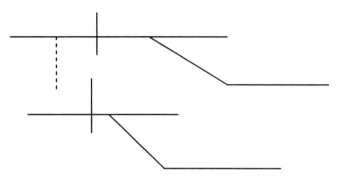

2. Every one **that is of the truth** heareth my voice. (John 18:37c)

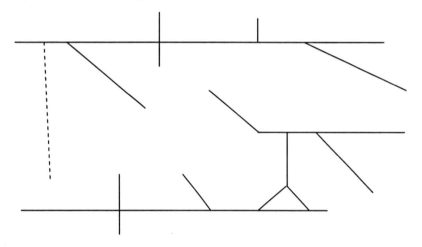

3. The LORD preserveth all them **that love him**. (Psalm 145:20a)

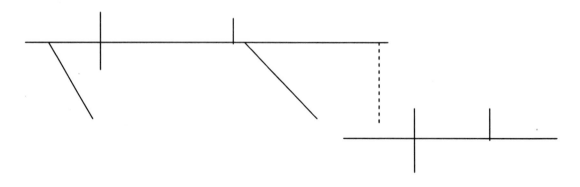

# Diagramming Adjective Clauses
## Practice Sheet

4. The grace of God that bringeth salvation hath appeared to all men. (Titus 2:11)

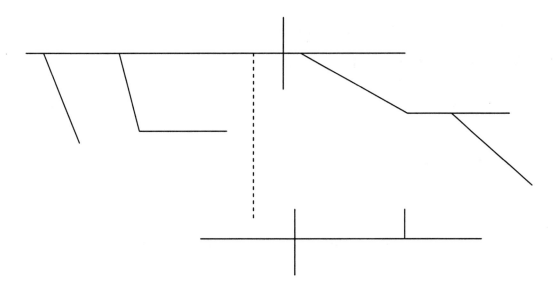

5. Every spirit that confesseth that Jesus Christ is come in the flesh is of God. (1 John 4:2b)

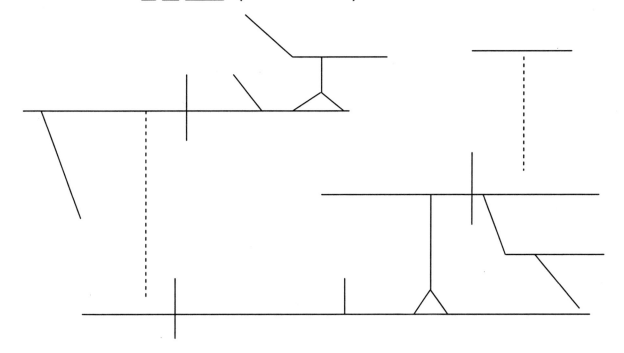

## Diagramming Adjective Clauses
### Directions for Test

First, diagram the independent clause, and then diagram the dependent clause *below* it. Draw a dotted line from the relative pronoun of the dependent clause to the word the clause modifies in the independent clause.

Example: He **that walketh uprightly** walketh surely.

(Proverbs 10:9a)

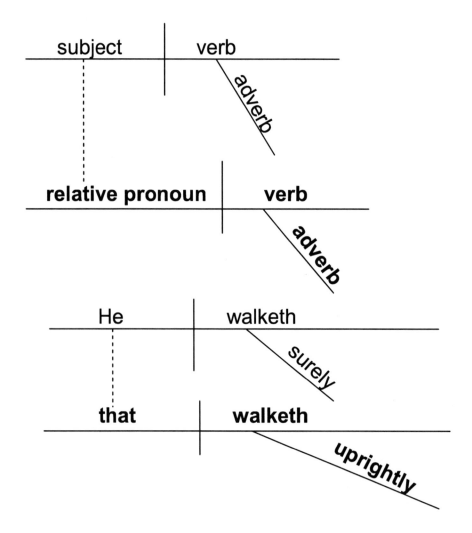

# Diagramming Adjective Clauses
## Test

1. He **that covereth his sins** shall not prosper.

   (Proverbs 28:13a)

2. A man **that hath friends** must shew himself friendly.

   (Proverbs 18:24a)

3. He **that hath pity upon the poor** lendeth unto the LORD.

   (Proverbs 19:17a)

4. The LORD is known by the judgment **which he executeth**.

   (Psalm 9:16a)

5. They **that deal truly** are his [God's] delight.

   (Proverbs 12:22b)

# 29 - Diagramming Adverb Clauses

An **adverb clause** is a group of words that has a subject and a predicate, and it modifies a verb, verb phrase, verbal, adjective, or adverb. It, a dependent clause, is linked to the independent clause by a subordinating conjunction.

| Subordinating Conjunctions | | | | |
|---|---|---|---|---|
| after | as long as | lest | that | when |
| although | because | since | though | where |
| as | before | so that | unless | whether |
| as if | if | than | until | while |

Like words and phrases, clauses can also be used as adverbs. Adverbial clauses answer these questions: "When?", "Where?", "Why?", "How?", and "To what extent?"

Directions:

Study the examples. The **adverb clause** is put in dark print. Look for the subordinating conjunction that introduces the clause. Read the explanation for each sentence.

## Diagramming Adverb Clauses
Explanation and Directions

1. The **adverb clause "Though I walk in the midst of trouble"** modifies the verb "wilt revive." "Though" is the subordinating conjunction.

2. **"When thou liest down"** is the **adverb clause** which modifies the verb "shalt be." The subordinating conjunction is the word "when."

3. **"When pride cometh"** is the **adverb clause** which modifies the verb "cometh." The subordinating conjunction is "When."

4. **"When the righteous are in authority"** is the **adverb clause** which modifies the verb "rejoice." The subordinating conjunction is "When."

5. **"When the wicked beareth rule"** is the **adverb clause** which modifies the verb "mourn." The subordinating conjunction is "When."

# Diagramming Adverb Clauses
## Examples

1. **Though I walk in the midst of trouble**, thou wilt revive me.
   (Psalm 138:7a)

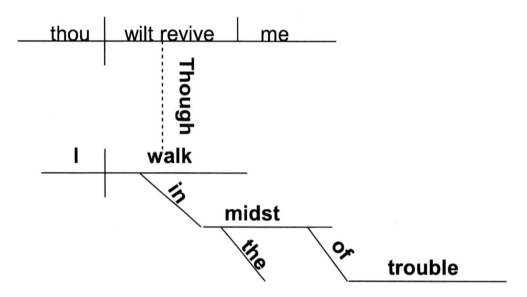

2. **When thou liest down**, thou shalt not be afraid.
   (Proverbs 3:24a)

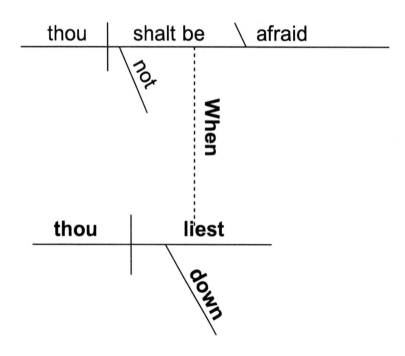

# Diagramming Adverb Clauses
## Examples

3. **When pride cometh**, then cometh shame. (Proverbs 11:2a)

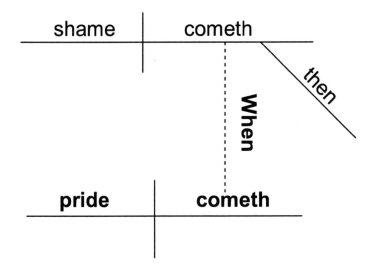

4. **When the righteous are in authority**, the people rejoice. (Proverbs 29:2a)

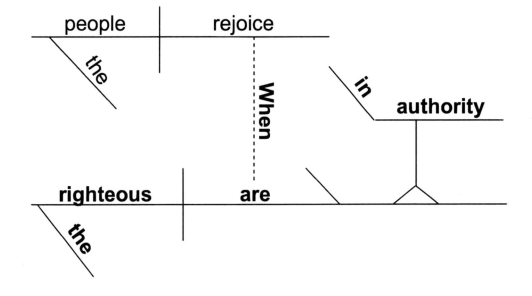

## Diagramming Adverb Clauses
## Examples

5. **When the wicked beareth rule**, the people mourn.
(Proverbs 29:2b)

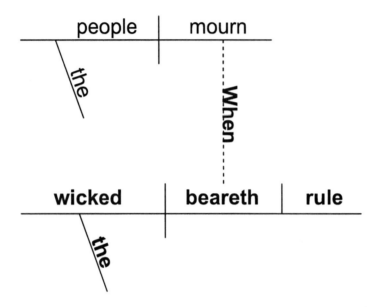

# Diagramming Adverb Clauses
Directions for Practice Sheets

Study the practice sentences. The independent clauses are underlined, and the dependent clauses (**adverb clauses**) are in dark print.

**Adverb clauses** answer the following questions: "When?", "Where?", "Why?", "How?", and "To what extent?"

The dependent clause is placed underneath the independent clause. The subordinating conjunction on a dotted line connects the dependent clause to the independent clause.

# Diagramming Adverb Clauses
## Practice Sheet

1. **When the wicked are multiplied**, transgression increaseth: but the righteous shall see their fall. (Proverbs 29:16)

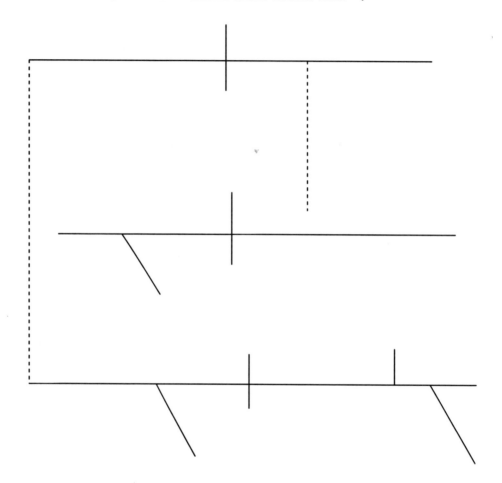

2. **If ye love me**, keep my commandments. (John 14:15)

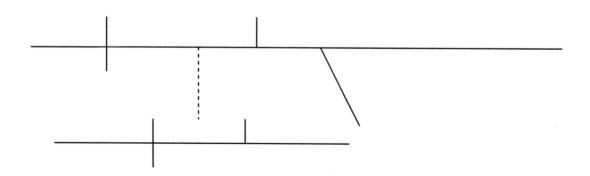

# Diagramming Adverb Clauses
## Practice Sheet

3. I will sing unto the LORD, **because he hath dealt bountifully with me**. (Psalm 13:6)

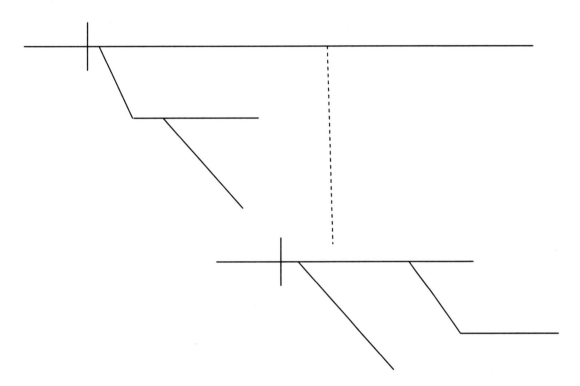

4. The wicked flee **when no man pursueth**. (Proverbs 28:1a)

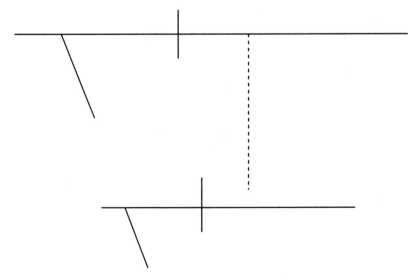

# Diagramming Adverb Clauses
## Practice Sheet

5. **Though the LORD be high**, yet hath he respect unto the lowly: but the proud he knoweth afar off. (Psalm 138:6)

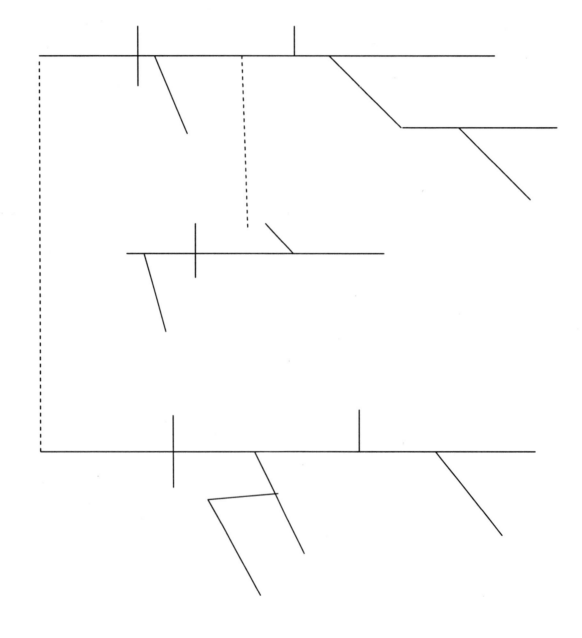

181

# Diagramming Adverb Clauses
## Directions for Test

Study the test sentences. Again, the independent clauses are underlined, and the **adverb clauses** are in dark print. Find the independent clause first for each sentence (the underlined words) and diagram it. Then diagram the **adverb clause** underneath the independent clause. Connect the **adverb clause** to the independent clause by drawing a dotted line with the subordinating conjunction on it from the verb in the **adverb clause** to the verb in the independent clause.

Example:

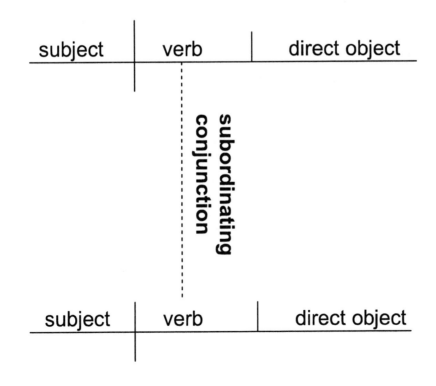

# Diagramming Adverb Clauses
## Test

1. I am the door: **by me if any man enter in**, he shall be saved. (John 10:9a)

2. Beloved, **if God so loved us**, we ought also to love one another. (1 John 4:11)

3. **When I became a man**, I put away childish things. (1 Corinthians 13:11b)

4. **While we were yet sinners**, Christ died for us. (Romans 5:8b)

5. **When the fulness of the time was come**, God sent forth his Son. (Galatians 4:4a)

## 30 - Unit 3
## Test

Directions: Diagram the following sentences:

1. I love the LORD, because he hath heard my voice and my supplications. (Psalm 116:1)

2. This is the day which the LORD hath made. (Psalm 118:24a)

3. I know, O LORD, that thy judgments are right. (Psalm 119:75a)

4. Happy is that people, whose God is the LORD. (Psalm 144:15b)

5. Rejoice not when thine enemy falleth. (Proverbs 24:17a)

# Unit 4

## Diagramming Sentence Types

31. **Diagramming Simple Sentences** .................... 186

32. **Diagramming Compound Sentences** ............ 193

33. **Diagramming Complex Sentences** ................ 200

34. **Unit 4 - Test** ....................................................... 212

## 31 - Diagramming Simple Sentences

A **simple sentence** contains one independent clause and has no dependent clauses. It makes complete sense in itself. It may have a compound subject or a compound verb or both, but it does not have two complete statements in it.

Directions - Study the examples. Each of the sentences is a **simple sentence**. That means all of the words in the sentence are in dark print and are to be diagrammed.

1. This sentence has a simple subject (*Father*) and a compound predicate (*loveth* and *hath given*), but it is not a compound sentence.
2. This sentence is a command and the understood subject is *you.*
3. This sentence has one subject and one verb, which makes it a **simple sentence**.
4. This sentence has one simple subject (*they*) and a compound verb (*shall turn* and *shall be turned*), so it is still a **simple sentence**.
5. Although the subject in this sentence has a number of adjectives, the **sentence** is still **simple**.

Directions for Practice Sheets

All of the words in the practice sheets are in dark print. Place all of them in the right places.

# Diagramming Simple Sentences
## Examples

1. **The Father loveth the Son, and hath given all things into his hand.** (John 3:35)

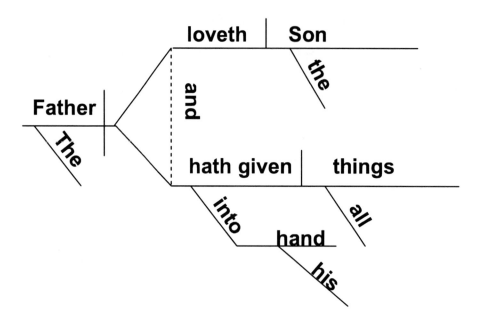

2. **Cast thy burden upon the LORD.** (Psalm 55:22a)

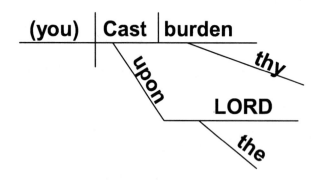

3. **Thy faith hath saved thee.** (Luke 7:50a)

# Diagramming Simple Sentences
## Examples

4. **They shall turn away their ears from the truth, and shall be turned unto fables.** (2 Timothy 4:4)

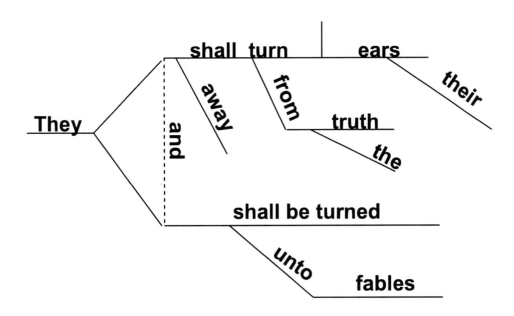

5. **The effectual fervent prayer of a righteous man availeth much.** (James 5:16b)

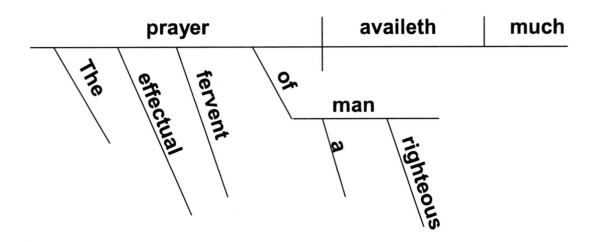

# Diagramming Simple Sentences
## Practice Sheet

1. **The LORD shall judge his people.** (Hebrews 10:30c)

2. **His name is called The Word of God.** (Revelation 19:13b)

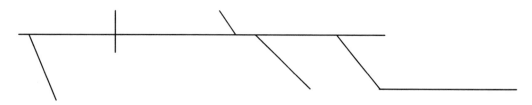

3. **A friend loveth at all times.** (Proverbs 17:17a)

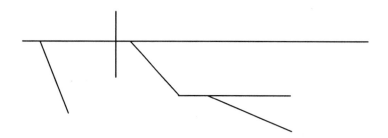

4. **A wise man feareth, and departeth from evil.** (Proverbs 14:16a)

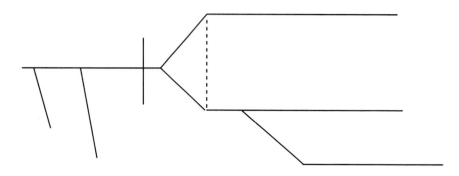

# Diagramming Simple Sentences
## Practice Sheet

5. **The Son of man shall come in the glory of his Father with his angels**. (Matthew 16:27a)

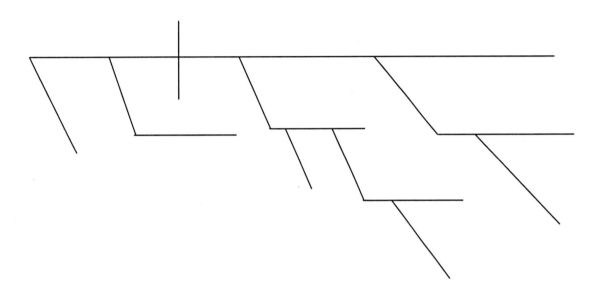

# Diagramming Simple Sentences
## Directions for Test

Diagram the test sentences. Sentence 5 has a prepositional phrase used as a predicate complement. A phrase used as a noun is called a *nominal*.

To diagram a prepositional phrase used as a predicate complement, draw a forked line on the *predicate complement* area of the base line. Place the prepositional phrase on the forked line.

Example:

The LORD is in his holy temple. (Habakkuk 2:20a)

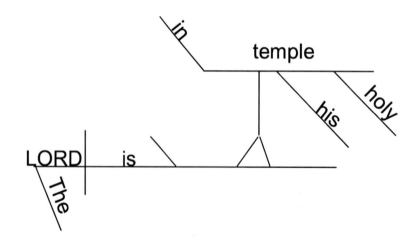

# Diagramming Simple Sentences
Test

1. **In the beginning God created the heaven and the earth.**
   (Genesis 1:1)
2. **I will confess my transgressions unto the LORD.**
   ( Psalm 32:5b)
3. **By the works of the law shall no flesh be justified.**
   (Galatians 2:16c)
4. **A merry heart doeth good like a medicine.**
   (Proverbs 17:22a)
5. **Death and life are in the power of the tongue.**
   (Proverbs 18:21a)

## 32 - Diagramming Compound Sentences

**Compound sentences** contain two independent clauses. A clause contains a subject and a verb. An independent clause can stand by itself. The two clauses are connected by a comma and a coordinating conjunction or by a colon or a comma. A colon or a comma was used in the KJV edition that I used, but I understand that later editions used the semi-colon as we do now.

| **Coordinating Conjunctions** |
|---|
| **and, or, for, nor, but, yet, so** |

Directions: Study the examples. If necessary, review the material on coordinating conjunctions.

Directions for Practice Pages:

1. Find the **coordinating conjunction** in the sentence.

2. Place it inside the dotted line on the side of the two independent clauses.

3. Fill in the blanks for the rest of the words.

# Diagramming Compound Sentences
## Examples

1. **Blessed are the pure in heart: for they shall see God.** (Matthew 5:8)

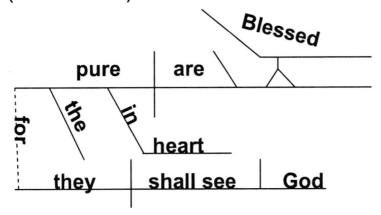

2. **Cast thy burden upon the LORD, and he shall sustain thee.** (Psalm 55:22a)

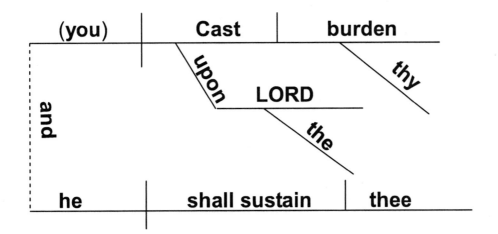

3. **Arise, and be not afraid.** (Matthew 17:7b)

# Diagramming Compound Sentences
## Examples

4. **Take my yoke upon you, and learn of me**. (Matthew 11:29a)

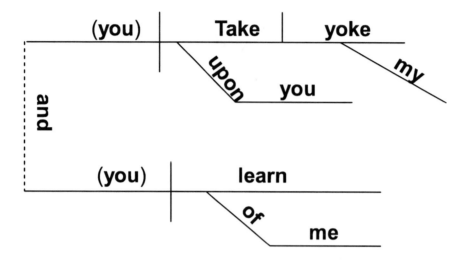

5. **I will not leave you** comfortless: **I will come to you**. (John 14:18)

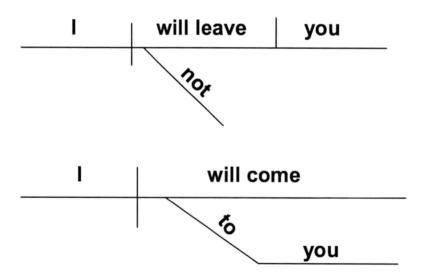

# Diagramming Compound Sentences - Practice Sheet

1. **Lord, shew us the Father, and it sufficeth us.** (John 14:8)

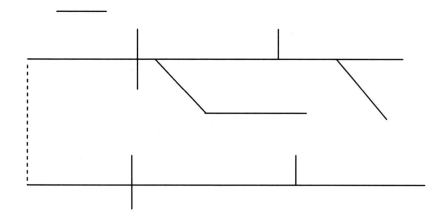

2. **He must increase, but I must decrease.** (John 3:30)

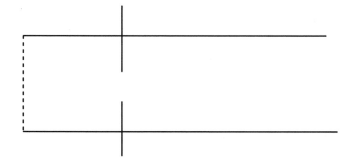

3. **My Father worketh hitherto, and I work.** (John 5:17)

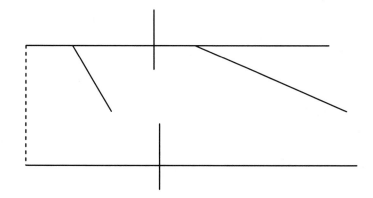

# Diagramming Compound Sentences - Practice Sheet

4. **Judge not according to the appearance, but judge righteous judgment.** (John 7:24) *According to* is a two-word preposition.

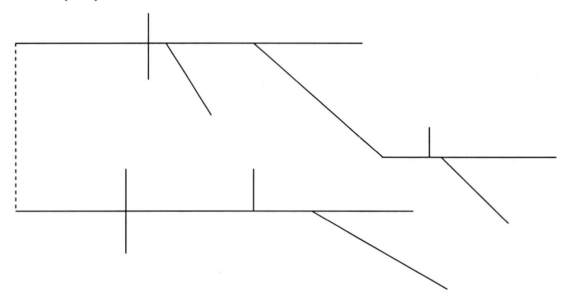

5. **I am crucified with Christ: nevertheless I live**; yet not I, but Christ liveth in me: and the life which I now live in the flesh I live by the faith of the Son of God, who loved me, and gave himself for me. (Galatians 2:20)

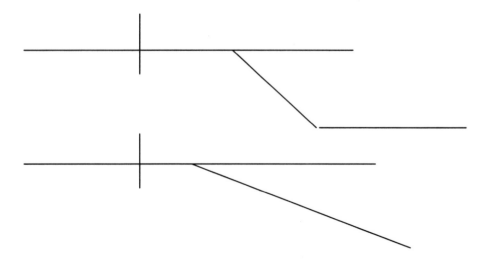

## Diagramming Compound Sentences
### Directions for Test

Each of the independent clauses is placed on its own base line. Draw a dotted line with the **coordinating conjunction** on top of it between the independent clauses. If there is no **coordinating conjunction**, do not connect the independent clauses. See examples below.

**Compound Sentence <u>with</u> a Coordinating Conjunction**

```
       subject    |    verb
_____|_____
:                 |
:c                |
:o                |
:o                |
:rd               |
:in               |
:at               |
:in               |
:g                |
:                 |
:                 |
       subject    |    verb
_____|_____
                  |
```

**Compound Sentence <u>without</u> a Coordinating Conjunction**

```
       subject    |    verb
_____|_____
                  |


       subject    |    verb
_____|_____
                  |
```

Diagram all the words in the sentences.

## Diagramming Compound Sentences
Test

1. **I believed, and therefore have I spoken.**

    (2 Corinthians 4:13b)

2. **Seek the LORD, and his strength: seek his face evermore.** (Psalm 105:4)

3. **I have fought a good fight, I have finished my course, I have kept the faith.** (2 Timothy 4:7)

4. **I was a stranger, and ye took me in.** (Matthew 25:35c)

5. **Awake to righteousness, and sin not.**

    (1 Corinthians 15:34a)

## 33 - Diagramming Complex Sentences

**Complex sentences** contain one independent clause and at least one dependent clause. A clause contains a subject and a verb. An independent clause can stand by itself. A dependent clause cannot. It is linked to the independent clause with a word(s) that relates it to the independent clause. **A dependent clause may be used as a noun, adjective, or an adverb.**

Directions: Study the examples. The independent clause is underlined, and the dependent clause is in dark print.

1. "Believe in the light" is an independent clause with the understood subject "you." **"While ye have light"** is a dependent clause with "while" as the linking word. The dependent clause is used as an adverb telling when to believe.

2. "Ye would love me" is the independent clause. **"If God were your Father"** is the dependent clause with the linking word "if." The dependent clause is used as an

## Diagramming Complex Sentences

adverb which modifies the verb "would love."

3. "<u>He</u> <u>hath</u> <u>everlasting</u> <u>life</u>" is the independent clause. "**That believeth on the Son**" is the dependent clause with the word "that" as the linking word. The dependent clause is used as an adjective which describes the pronoun "he."

4. "<u>The</u> <u>Father</u> <u>himself</u> <u>loveth</u> <u>you</u>" is the independent clause. "**Because ye have loved me**" is the dependent clause with "because" as the linking word. The dependent clause is used as an adverb to modify the verb "loveth."

5. "<u>I</u> <u>know</u>" is the independent clause. "**Whom I have believed**" is the dependent clause. The dependent clause is used as a direct object because it answers the question "What?" after the action verb "know."

# Diagramming Complex Sentences
## Examples

1. **While ye have light,** <u>believe in the light</u>. (John 12:36a)

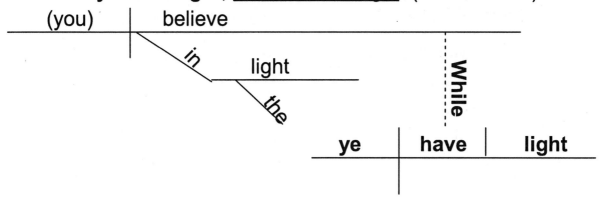

2. **If God were your Father**, <u>ye would love me</u>. (John 8:42a)

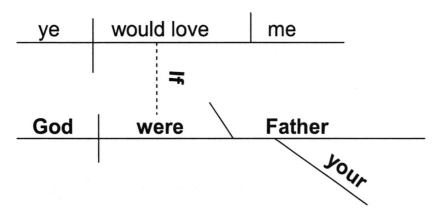

3. <u>He</u> **that believeth on the Son** <u>hath everlasting life.</u> (John 3:36a)

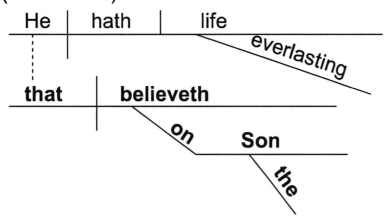

# Diagramming Complex Sentences
## Examples

4. The Father himself loveth you, **because ye have loved me**. (John 16:27a)

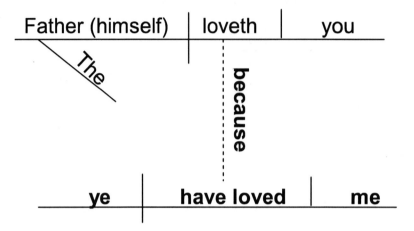

5. I know **whom I have believed**. (2 Timothy 1:12b)

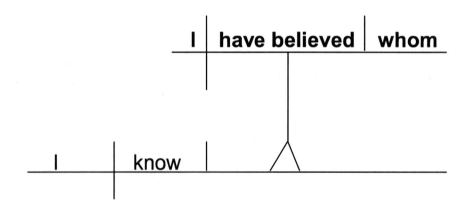

## Diagramming Complex Sentences
Directions for Practice Sheets

For each of the sentences do the following:

1. Fill in the blanks for the independent clause first.

2. Fill in the blanks for the dependent clause.

3. Make the dependent clause used as an adjective modify a noun.

4. Make the dependent clause used as an adverb modify a verb, adjective, or another adverb.

5. Make the dependent clause used as a noun take the place of a subject, indirect object, direct object, predicate complement, or appositive.

# Diagramming Complex Sentences
## Practice Sheet

1. **If any man thirst,** let him come unto me, and drink. (John 7:37b)

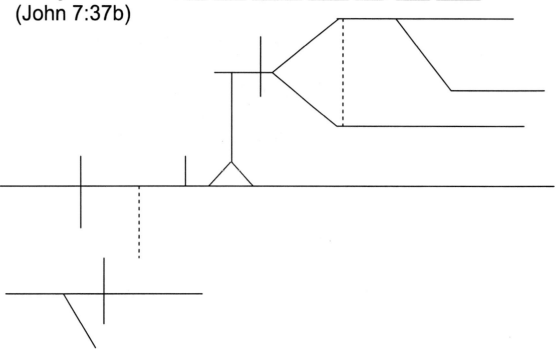

2. The grace of God **that bringeth salvation** hath appeared to all men. (Titus 2:11)

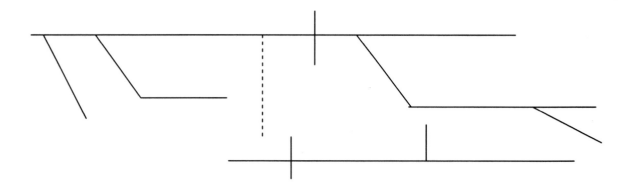

# Diagramming Complex Sentences
## Practice Sheet

3. <u>Provide</u> <u>me</u> <u>now</u> <u>a</u> <u>man</u> **that can play well**. (1 Samuel 16:17a)

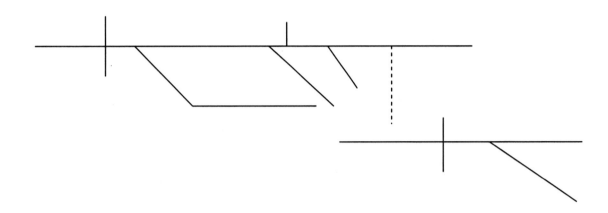

4. <u>He</u> **that trusteth in his riches** <u>shall</u> <u>fall</u>. (Proverbs 11:28a)

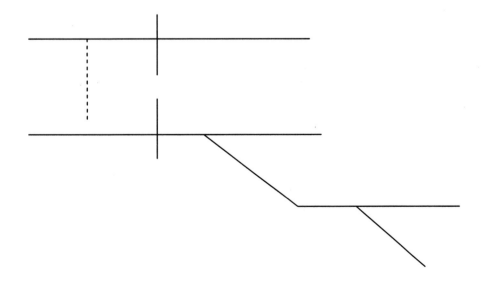

# Diagramming Complex Sentences
## Practice Sheet

5. Every one that is proud in heart is an abomination to the LORD. (Proverbs 16:5a)

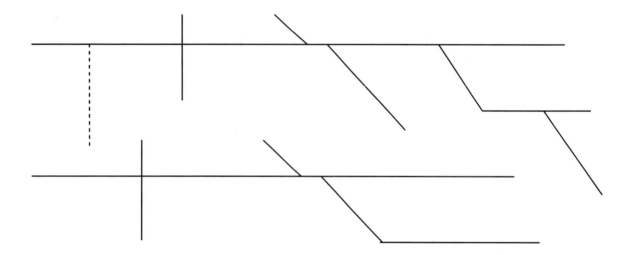

# Diagramming Complex Sentences
## Directions for Test

For **complex sentences** with an adjective clause (dependent),

1. Diagram the independent clause first.
2. Diagram the dependent adjective clause as you would an independent clause.
3. Show how the clauses are related by drawing a dotted line from the linking word in the dependent clause to the word that it refers to in the independent clause.

For **complex sentences** with an adverbial clause (dependent),

1. Diagram the independent clause first.
2. Diagram the dependent adverbial clause as you would an independent clause.
3. Remember that an adverbial clause answers the same question that an adverb would answer.
4. Write the joining word (subordinating conjunction) on the dotted line between the two verbs.

For **complex sentences** with a noun clause (dependent),

1. Diagram the independent clause first.
2. Diagram the noun clause just as you would an independent clause.
3. Place the noun clause on a horizontal line above a vertical line with forked lines at its base.
4. Put the noun clause wherever it takes a noun's place.

# Diagramming Complex Sentences
## Directions for Test

Diagram the independent clause first (the one that is underlined). Then diagram the dependent clause underneath it. Connect the two clauses with the linking word. The following examples will show you where to connect the two clauses.

## Adjective Clause

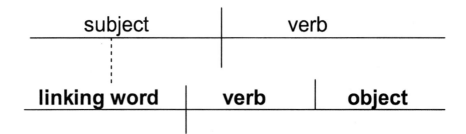

## Adverb Clause

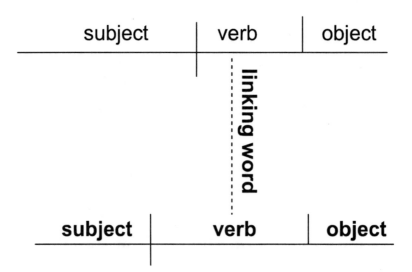

# Diagramming Complex Sentences
Directions for Test

## Noun Clause

Diagram the **noun clause** on a horizontal line placed above the base line. It is supported by a vertical line placed on forked lines which attach to the base line.

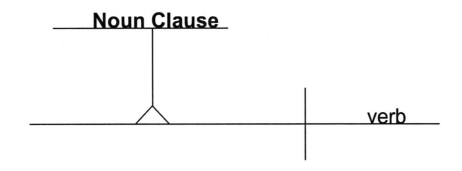

Some **noun clauses** have a signal word "that." If "that" is understood, use "(x)" to show that it is not actually in the sentence.

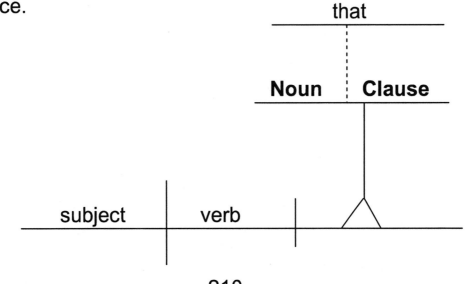

# Diagramming Complex Sentences
## Test

1. He that hearkeneth unto counsel is wise.

   (Proverbs 12:15b)

2. A man that hath friends must shew himself friendly.

   (Proverbs 18:24a)

3. The wicked flee when no man pursueth. (Proverbs 28:1a)

4. If a house be divided against itself, that house cannot stand.

   (Mark 3:25)

5. I know that my redeemer liveth. (Job 19:25a)

# 34 - Unit 4
## Test

Directions: Diagram the following sentences:

1. Gracious is the LORD, and righteous; yea, our God is merciful. (Psalm 116:5)
2. To depart from evil is understanding. (Job 28:28b)
3. Behold, the fear of the LORD, that is wisdom. (Job 28:28a)
4. I, even I, am the LORD; and beside me there* is no saviour. (Isaiah 43:11)
5. If any man be in Christ, he is a new creature. (2 Corinthians 5:17a)

*The word "there" in the fourth sentence is a word that does not have any function in the sentence. It is called an expletive.

In diagramming, place it on a horizontal line but do not connect it to the rest of the sentence.

Example: There are sixty-six books in the Bible.

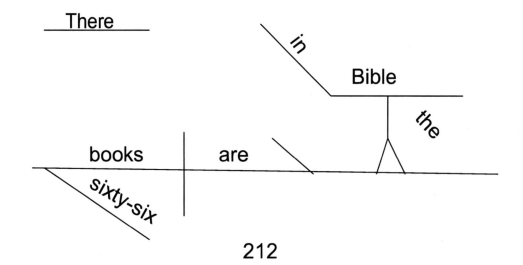

# Unit 5

## 35 - Test of all Units

Diagram each of the following sentences:

1. The entrance of thy words giveth light; it giveth understanding unto the simple. (Psalm 119:130)

2. He that is of a merry heart hath a continual feast. (Proverbs 15:15b)

3. Great and marvellous are thy works, Lord God Almighty. (Revelation 15:3b)

4. My brethren, count it all joy when ye fall into divers temptations. (James 1:2) Omit *all joy - objective complement.*

5. My grace is sufficient for thee: for my strength is made perfect in weakness. (2 Corinthians 12:9a)

6. A virtuous woman is a crown to her husband. (Proverbs 12:4a)

7. Ye do err, not knowing the scriptures, nor the power of God. (Matthew 22:29b)

8. Be ye therefore ready also: for the Son of man cometh at an hour when ye think not. (Luke 12:40)

9. The words of a wise man's mouth are gracious. (Ecclesiastes 10:12a)

10. A soft answer turneth away wrath. (Proverbs 15:1a)

11. Rejoice not when thine enemy falleth. (Proverbs 24:17a)

## Test of all Units

12. Heaven and earth shall pass away, but my words shall not pass away. (Matthew 24:35)

13. A man that hath friends must shew himself friendly. (Proverbs 18:24a)

14. God so loved the world, that he gave his only begotten Son, that whosoever believeth in him should not perish, but have everlasting life. (John 3:16)

15. Choose you this day whom ye will serve. (Joshua 24:15b)

16. I, even I, am he that comforteth you. (Isaiah 51:12a)

17. Honour thy father and thy mother. (Exodus 20:12a)

18. With what judgment ye judge, ye shall be judged: and with what measure ye mete, it shall be measured to you again. (Matthew 7:2)

19. I have manifested thy name unto the men which thou gavest me out of the world. (John 17:6a)

20. I have finished the work which thou gavest me to do. (John 17:4b)

# ANSWERS

# Unit 1 - 3

## Subject + Verb Sentence Pattern - Practice Answers

1. **Abraham tithed**. (Genesis 14:20)

   | Abraham | tithed |
   |---------|--------|

2. **Sarah laughed.** (Genesis 18:12)

   | Sarah | laughed |
   |-------|---------|

3. **Hagar fled.** (Genesis 16:6)

   | Hagar | fled |
   |-------|------|

4. **Isaac married.** (Genesis 24:67)

   | Isaac | married |
   |-------|---------|

5. **Esau bargained.** (Genesis 25:33)

   | Esau | bargained |
   |------|-----------|

# 3
## Subject + Verb Sentence Pattern - Test Answers

1. **Jacob lied**. (Genesis 27:19)

2. **Joseph forgave**. (Genesis 50:16-21)

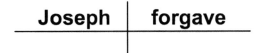

3. **Judah compromised**. (Genesis 37:26-27)

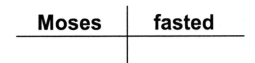

4. **Moses fasted**. (Exodus 34:28)

```
   Moses   |   fasted
_____|_____
           |
```

5. **Aaron obeyed**. (Exodus 7:6)

```
   Aaron   |   obeyed
_____|_____
           |
```

# 6  Subject + Verb + Direct Object Sentence Pattern

## Practice Answers

1. A merry heart doeth **good** like a medicine. (Proverbs 17:22a)

   ```
      heart   |  doeth  |  good
   ```

2. Every wise woman buildeth her **house**. (Proverbs 14:1a)

   ```
      woman   |  buildeth  |  house
   ```

3. A righteous man regardeth the **life** of his beast. (Proverbs 12:10a)

4. The **meek** will he guide in judgment. (Psalm 25:9a)

   ```
      he   |  will guide  |  meek
   ```

5. The LORD loveth the **righteous**. (Psalm 146:8c)

   ```
      LORD   |  loveth  |  righteous
   ```

# 6 - <u>Subject</u> + <u>Verb</u> + **Direct Object** Sentence Pattern

## Test Answers

1. The <u>LORD</u> <u>taketh</u> **pleasure** in his people. (Psalm 149:4a)

```
 LORD |  taketh  | pleasure
      |
```

2. The <u>LORD</u> <u>openeth</u> the **eyes** of the blind. (Psalm 146:8a)

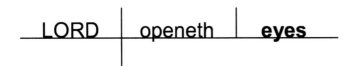

3. <u>He</u> <u>shall cover</u> **thee** with his feathers. (Psalm 91:4a)

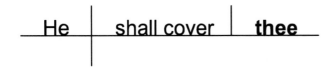

4. <u>He</u> <u>appointed</u> the **moon** for seasons. (Psalm 104:19a)

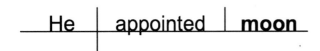

5. <u>God</u> <u>setteth</u> the **solitary** in families. (Psalm 68:6a)

```
 God  |  setteth  | solitary
      |
```

## 7 - <u>Subject</u> + <u>Verb</u> + **Indirect Object** + <u>Direct Object</u>

## Sentence Pattern - Practice Answers

1. The <u>God</u> of Israel <u>grant</u> **thee** thy <u>petition</u>. (I Samuel 1:17b)

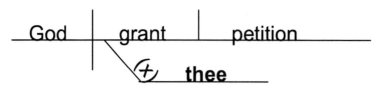

2. <u>I</u> <u>will pay</u> **thee** my <u>vows</u>. (Psalm 66:13b)

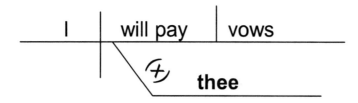

3. <u>I</u> <u>will give</u> **you** the sure <u>mercies</u> of David. (Acts 13:34b)

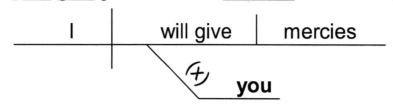

4. <u>I</u> <u>made</u> **me** great <u>works</u>. (Ecclesiastes 2:4a)

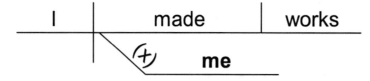

5. The <u>king</u> <u>granted</u> **him** all his <u>request</u>. (Ezra 7:6c)

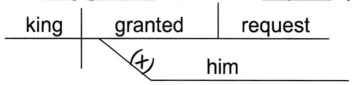

# 7 - <u>Subject</u> + <u>Verb</u> + **Indirect Object** + <u>Direct Object</u>

## Sentence Pattern - Test Answers

1. <u>I</u> <u>have provided</u> **me** a <u>king</u> among his sons. (1 Samuel 16:1d)

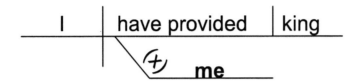

2. <u>Thou</u> <u>shalt</u> not <u>make</u> **thee** any graven <u>image</u>. (Deuteronomy 5:8a)

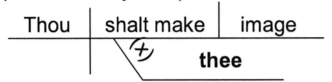

3. The <u>LORD</u> <u>will build</u> **thee** an <u>house</u>. (1 Chronicles 17:10c)

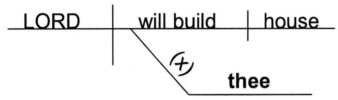

4. <u>He</u> <u>shall send</u> **them** a <u>saviour</u>. (Isaiah 19:20c)

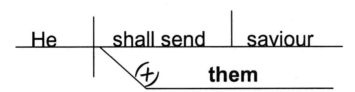

5. <u>God</u> <u>will provide</u> **himself** a <u>lamb</u> for a burnt offering. (Genesis 22:8a)

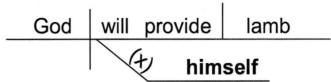

# 9 - Subject + Linking Verb + Predicate Complement

## Sentence Pattern - Practice Answers

1. I **am** the **door**. (John 10:9a)

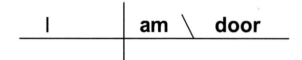

2. I **am** the true **vine**. (John 15:1a)

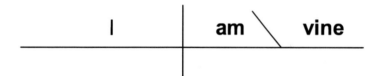

3. I **am** the living **bread.** (John 6:51a)

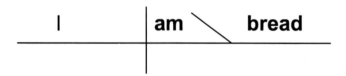

4. This **is** my beloved **Son**. (Luke 9:35b)

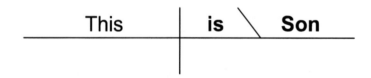

5. He **was** a burning and a shining **light**. (John 5:35a)

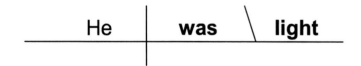

# 9 - Subject + Linking Verb + Predicate Complement

## Sentence Pattern

## Test Answers

1. The LORD is my shepherd. (Psalm 23:1a)

   LORD | is \ shepherd

2. Sin is the transgression of the law. (1 John 3:4b)

   Sin | is \ transgression

3. We are labourers together with God. (1 Corinthians 3:9a)

   We | are \ labourers

4. Ye are God's husbandry. (1 Corinthians 3:9b)

   Ye | are \ husbandry

5. Ye are God's building. (1 Corinthians 3:9c)

   Ye | are \ building

## 11 - <u>Subject</u> + <u>Linking Verb</u> + **Predicate Adjective**

## Sentence Pattern - Practice Answers

1. The <u>LORD</u> <u>is</u> **good.** (Psalm 135:3b)

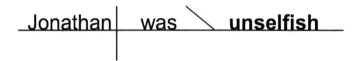

2. <u>Jonathan</u>, Saul's son, <u>was</u> **unselfish.** (1 Samuel 18:3-4)

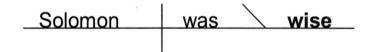

3. <u>Solomon</u> <u>was</u> **wise**. (1 Kings 3:12)

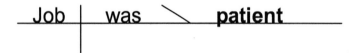

4. <u>Job</u> <u>was</u> **patient**. (James 5:11a)

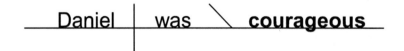

5. <u>Daniel</u> <u>was</u> **courageous**. (Daniel 1:1-8)

Daniel | was \ **courageous**

# 11 - <u>Subject</u> + <u>Linking Verb</u> + **Predicate Adjective**

## Sentence Pattern - Test Answers

1. Thy <u>testimonies</u> <u>are</u> very **sure**. (Psalm 93:5a)

       testimonies | are \ sure

2. The <u>LORD</u> <u>is</u> **worthy** to be praised. (Psalm 18:3b)

       LORD | is \ worthy

3. Thy <u>mercy</u> <u>is</u> **great** unto the heavens. (Psalm 57:10a)

       mercy | is \ great

4. The <u>righteous</u> <u>shall be</u> **glad** in the LORD. (Psalm 64:10a)

       righteous | shall be \ glad

5. <u>Esther</u> <u>was</u> **loyal** to God and her people. (Esther 4:15-16)

       Esther | was \ loyal

## 12 - Subject "You" Understood

Sentence Pattern - Practice Answers

1. Search the scriptures. (John 5:39a)

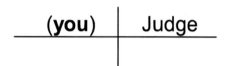

2. Judge not according to the appearance. (John 7:24a)

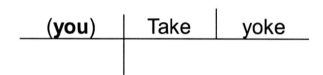

3. Take my yoke upon you. (Matthew 11:29a)

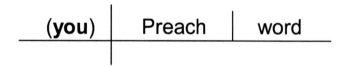

4. Preach the word. (2 Timothy 4:2a)

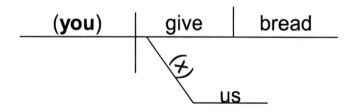

5. Lord, evermore give us this bread. (John 6:34b)

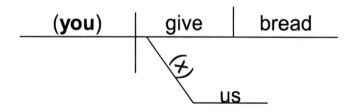

## 12 - **Subject "You" Understood**

## Sentence Pattern - Test Answers

1. <u>Order</u> my <u>steps</u> in thy word. (Psalm 119:133a)

   | **(you)** | Order | steps |

2. <u>Rebuke</u> not an <u>elder</u>. (1 Timothy 5:1a)

   | **(you)** | Rebuke | elder |

3. <u>Come</u> unto me. (Matthew 11:28a)

   | **(you)** | Come |

4. <u>Rejoice</u> in the LORD. (Psalm 33:1a)

   | **(you)** | Rejoice |

5. <u>Deliver</u> <u>me</u> in thy righteousness. (Psalm 71:2a)

   | **(you)** | Deliver | me |

## 13 - Unit 1 - Test Answers

1. **God is** our **refuge** and strength, a very present help in trouble. (Psalm 46:1)

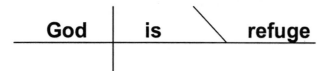

2. **Thou shalt make thee** no molten **gods**. (Exodus 34:17)

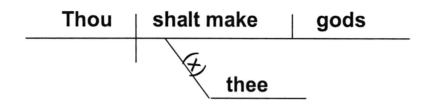

3. **Remember** the sabbath **day**, to keep it holy. (Exodus 20:8)

| (thou) | **Remember** | day |
|---|---|---|

4. The **testimony** of the LORD **is sure**, making wise the simple. (Psalm 19:7b)

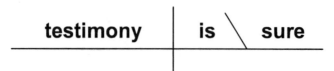

5. My **soul thirsteth** for God, for the living God. (Psalm 42:2a)

| soul | thirsteth |
|---|---|

Unit 2 - 14

## Prepositional Phrases - Practice Answers

1. Be not wise in your own conceits. (Romans 12:16c)

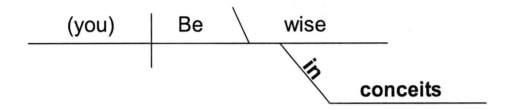

2. Love worketh no ill to his neighbor. (Romans 13:10a)

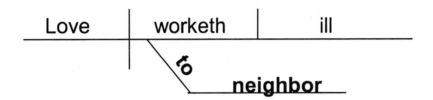

3. Pray without ceasing. (1 Thessalonians 5:17)

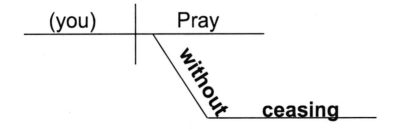

# 14 - **Prepositional Phrases** - Practice Answers

4. **In** every **thing** give thanks. (1 Thessalonians 5:18a)

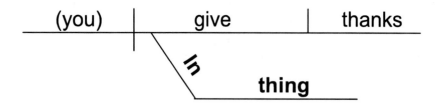

5. They parted my garments **among them**. (Matthew 27:35b)

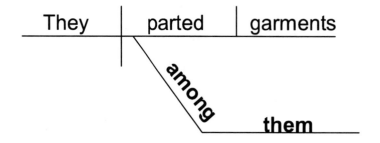

## 14 - **Prepositional Phrases** - Test Answers

1. The <u>love</u> **of money** <u>is</u> the <u>root</u> **of** all **evil**. (1 Timothy 6:10a)

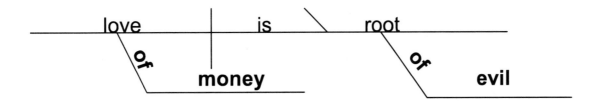

2. A double minded <u>man</u> <u>is</u> <u>unstable</u> **in** all his **ways**. (James 1:8)

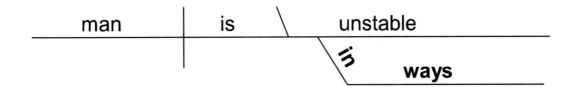

3. <u>Follow</u> **after charity**. (1 Corinthians 14:1a)

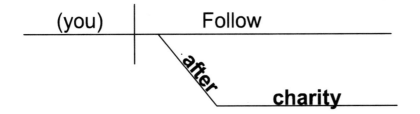

## 14 - **Prepositional Phrases** - Test Answers

4. The love **of Christ** constraineth us. (2 Corinthians 5:14a)

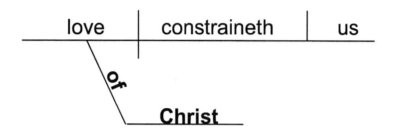

5. I am crucified **with Christ**: nevertheless I live; yet not I, but Christ liveth in me: and the life which I now live in the flesh I live by the faith of the Son of God, who loved me, and gave himself for me. (Galatians 2:20)

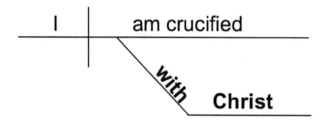

## 15 - **Direct Adjectives** - Practice Answers

1. <u>Ye</u> <u>are</u> **God's** <u>building.</u> (1 Corinthians 3:9c)

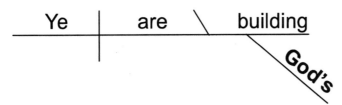

2. **The parched** <u>ground</u> <u>shall become</u> **a** <u>pool</u>. (Isaiah 35:7a)

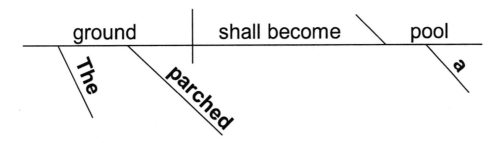

3. **The** <u>words</u> of **the** <u>LORD</u> <u>are</u> **pure** <u>words</u>. (Psalm 12:6a)

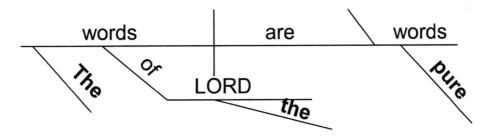

4. <u>Thou</u> <u>art</u> **my hiding** <u>place</u>. (Psalm 32:7a)

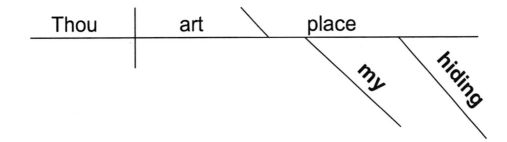

## 15 - **Direct Adjectives** - Practice Answers

5. **A virtuous** woman **is a** crown **to her** husband.
   (Proverbs 12:4a)

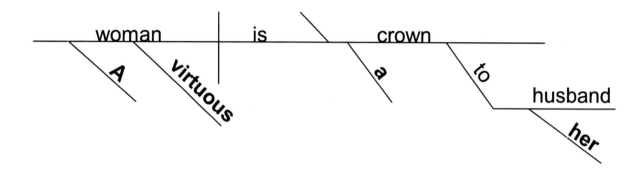

## 15 - **Direct Adjectives** - Test Answers

1. I hate **every false** way. (Psalm 119:104b)

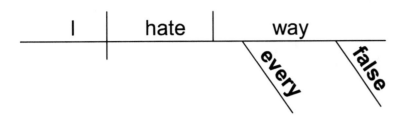

2. I have loved thee with **an everlasting** love. (Jeremiah 31:3b)

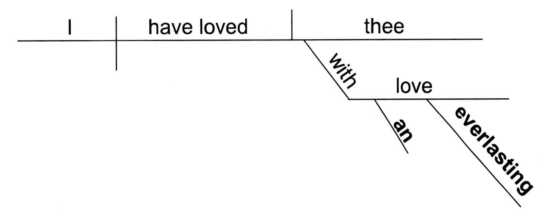

3. Make **no** friendship with **an angry** man. (Proverbs 22:24a)

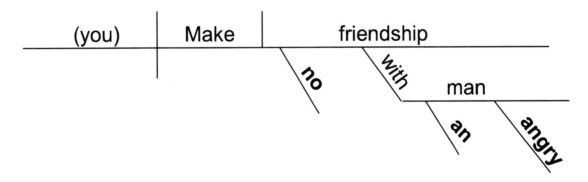

4. **His merciful** kindness is great toward us. (Psalm 117:2a)

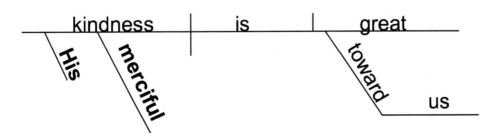

## 15 - **Direct Adjectives** - Test Answers

5. **The just** man walketh in **his** integrity. (Proverbs 20:7a)

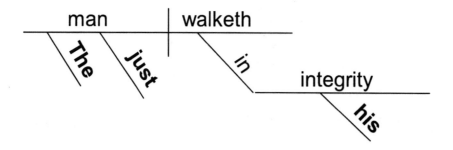

## 16 - **Participles** - Practice Answers

1. **Lying** lips are abomination to the LORD. (Proverbs 12:22a)

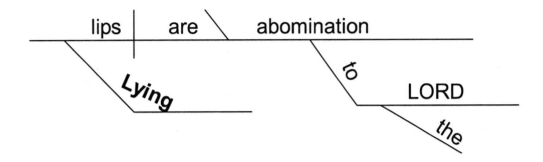

2. Hope **deferred** maketh the heart sick. (Proverbs 13:12a)

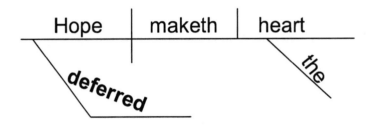

3. From whence then hast thou that **living** water? (John 4:11c)

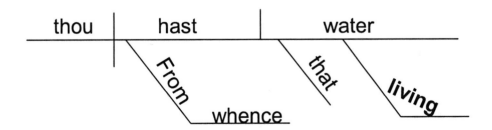

## 16 - **Participles** - Practice Answers

4. My son, God will provide himself a lamb for a **burnt** offering. (Genesis 22:8a)

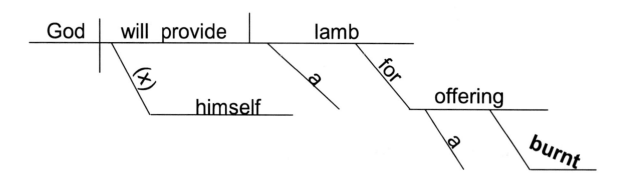

5. When he hath found it, he layeth it on his shoulders, **rejoicing**. (Luke 15:5)

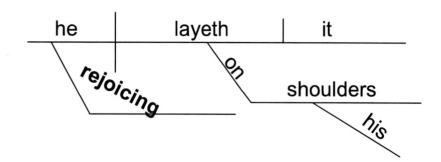

# 16 - **Participles** - Test Answers

1. The child grew, and waxed strong in spirit, **filled** with wisdom. (Luke 2:40a)

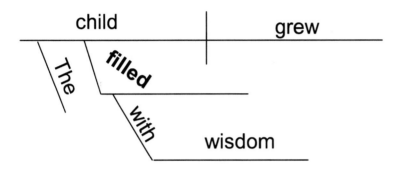

2. The statutes of the LORD are right, **rejoicing the heart**. (Psalm 19:8a)

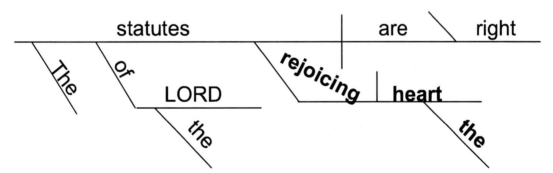

3. The commandment of the LORD is pure, **enlightening the eyes**. (Psalm 19:8b)

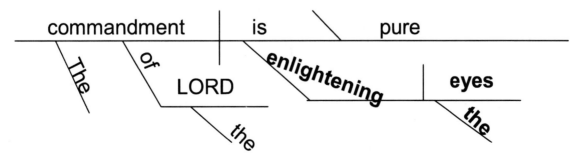

## 16 - **Participles** - Test Answers

4. The law of the LORD is perfect, **converting the soul**.
   (Psalm 19:7a)

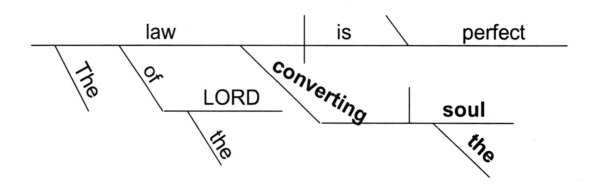

5. The testimony of the LORD is sure, **making** wise **the simple**.
   (Psalm 19:7b)

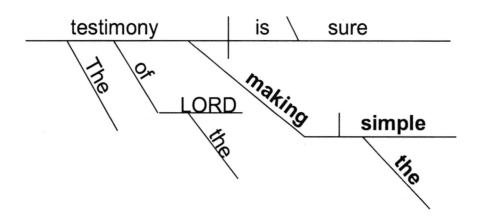

# 18 - Adverbs - Practice Answers

1. **How** sweet are thy words unto my taste! (Psalm 119:103a)

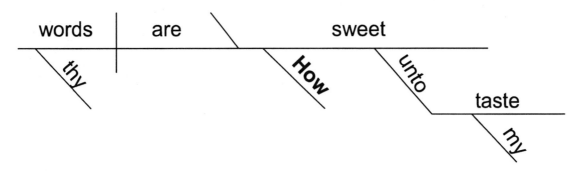

2. I have set the LORD **always** before me. (Psalm 16:8a)

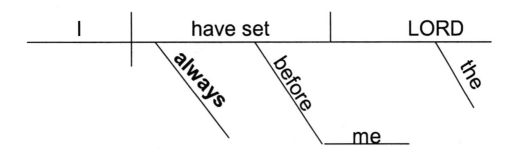

3. Ye can**not** serve God and mammon. (Luke 16:13c)

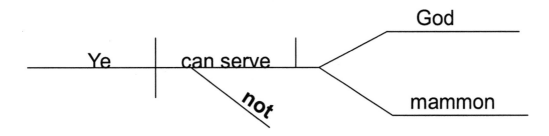

# 18 - **Adverbs** - Practice Answers

4. Seek ye **first** the kingdom of God, and his righteousness. (Matthew 6:33a)

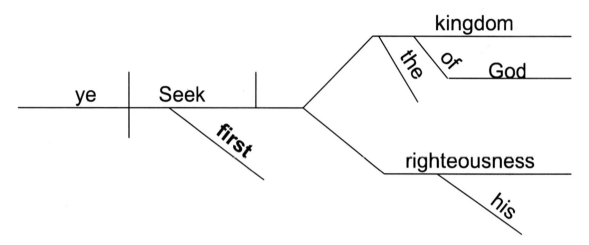

5. In him dwelleth all the fullness of the Godhead **bodily**. (Colossians 2:9)

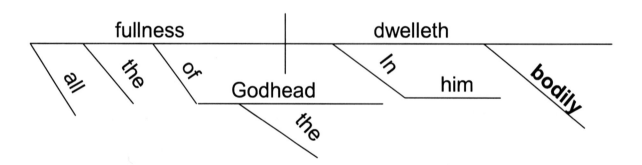

# 18 - **Adverbs** - Test Answers

1. My feet were **almost** gone; my steps had **well nigh** slipped. (Psalm 73:2b)

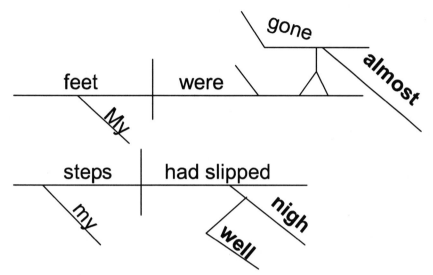

2. The very God of peace sanctify you **wholly**. (1 Thessalonians 5:23a)

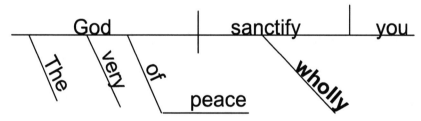

3. Some have entertained angels **unawares**. (Hebrews 13:2b)

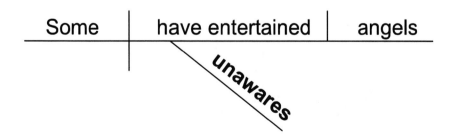

## 18 - **Adverbs** -Test Answers

4. Heaven and earth shall pass **away**, but my words shall **not** pass **away**. (Matthew 24:35)

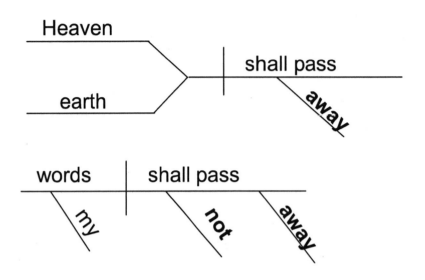

5. Draw **nigh** to God, and he will draw **nigh** to you. (James 4:8a)

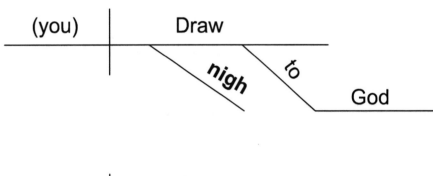

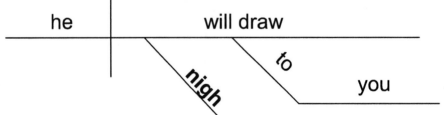

## 19 - Interjections - Practice Answers

1. **Behold,** I stand at the door, and knock. (Revelation 3:20a)

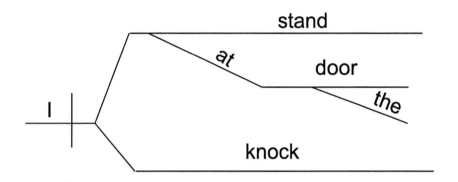

2. **Yea,** I will help thee. (Isaiah 41:10c)

Yea

```
    I   |  will help  |  thee
_____|_____|_____
```

3. **Behold**, what manner of love the Father hath bestowed upon us. (1 John 3:1a)

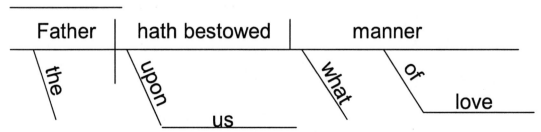

## 19 - **Interjections** - Test Answers

1. **Yea**, I will uphold thee with the right hand of my righteousness. (Isaiah 41:10d)

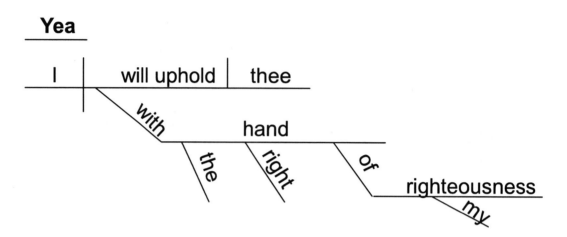

2. **Yea**, happy is that people, whose God is the LORD. (Psalm 144:15b)

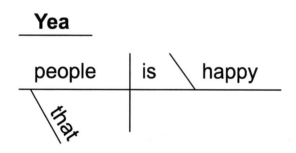

3. **Behold**, I make all things new. (Revelation 21:5b)

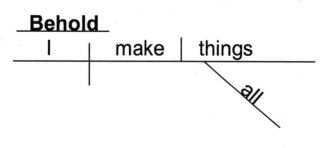

# 20 - **Conjunctions** - Practice Answers

1. He will not always chide: **neither** will he keep his anger for ever. (Psalm 103:9)

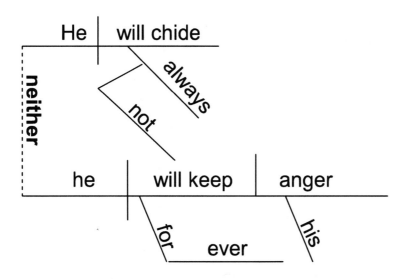

2. Behold, he that keepeth Israel shall **neither** slumber **nor** sleep. (Psalm 121:4)

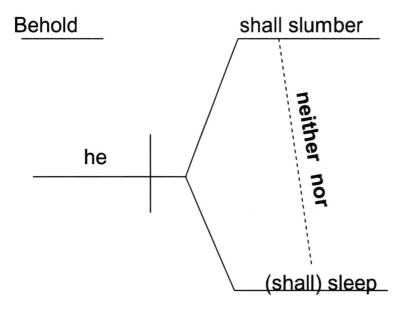

## 20 - **Conjunctions** - Practice Answers

3. The LORD knoweth the way of the righteous: **but** the way of the ungodly shall perish. (Psalm 1:6)

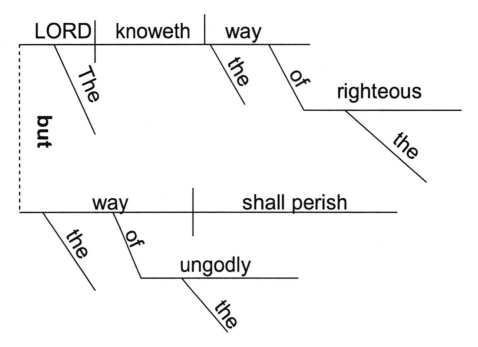

4. I will fear no evil: **for** thou art with me. (Psalm 23:4b)

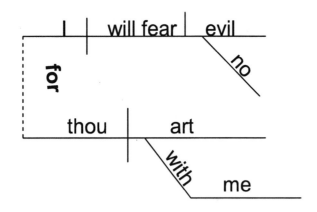

## 20 - **Conjunctions** - Practice Answers

5. Thou shalt call his name JESUS: **for** he shall save his people from their sins. (Matthew 1:21b)

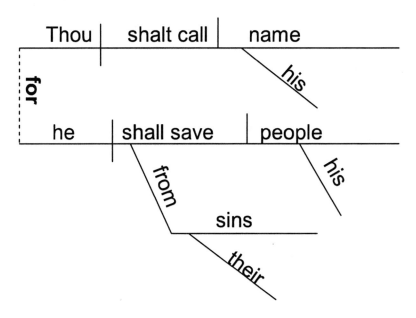

## 20 - **Conjunctions** - Test Answers

1. They have ears, **but** they hear not. (Psalm 135:17a)

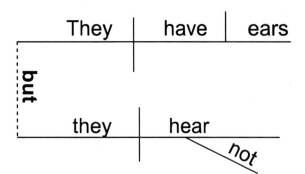

2. **Neither** fear ye their fear, **nor** be afraid. (Isaiah 8:12b)

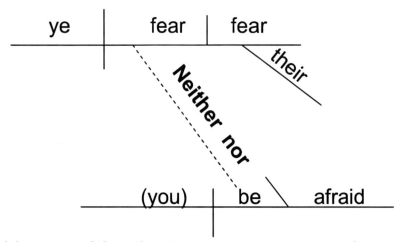

3. I have **neither** lent on usury, **nor** men have lent to me on usury. (Jeremiah 15:10b)

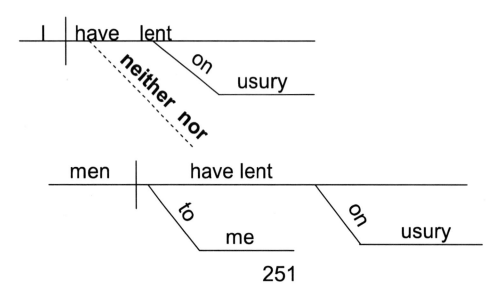

# 20 - **Conjunctions** - Test Answers

4. I laid me down **and** slept; I awaked; **for** the LORD sustained me. (Psalm 3:5)

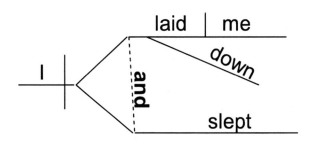

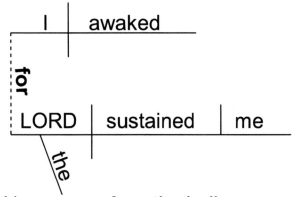

5. Heaven **and** earth shall pass away: **but** my words shall not pass away. (Luke 21:33)

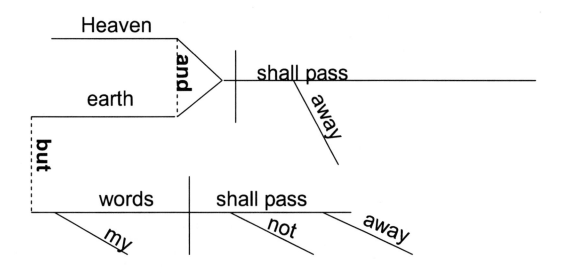

# 21 - **Pronouns** - Practice Answers

1. The LORD revealed **himself** to Samuel in Shiloh by the word of the LORD. (1 Samuel 3:21)

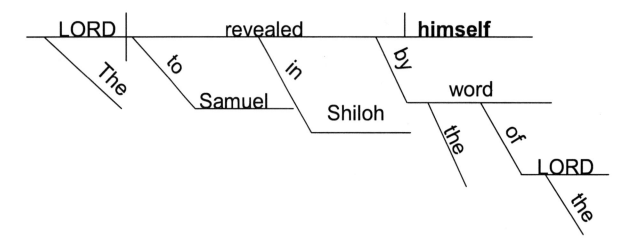

2. **I** thought on **my** ways, and turned **my** feet unto **thy** testimonies. (Psalm 119:59)

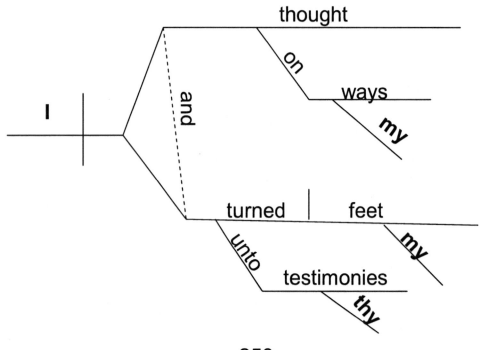

## 21 - **Pronouns** - Practice Answers

3. For **thy** name's sake, O LORD, pardon **mine** iniquity; for **it** is great. (Psalm 25:11)

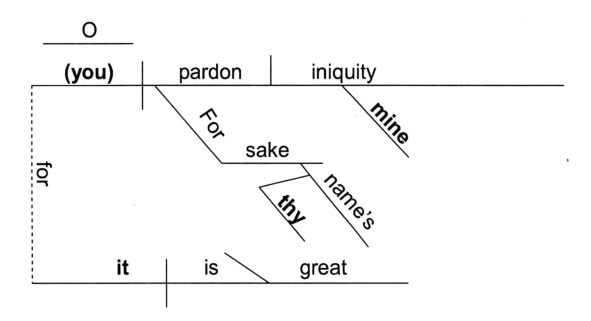

4. **He** [the LORD] brought **them** out of darkness and the shadow of death. (Psalm 107:14a)

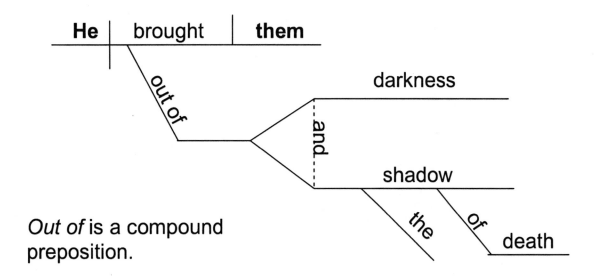

*Out of* is a compound preposition.

## 21 - **Pronouns** - Practice Answers

5. Nevertheless I am continually with thee: **thou** hast holden **me** by **my** right hand. (Psalm 73:23b)

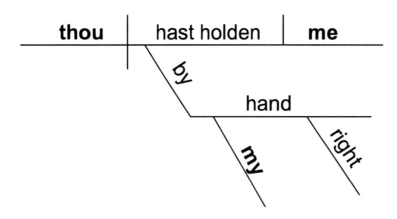

# 21 - **Pronouns** - Test Answers

1. [**you**, the LORD] O visit **me** with **thy** salvation. (Psalm 106:4b)

   O

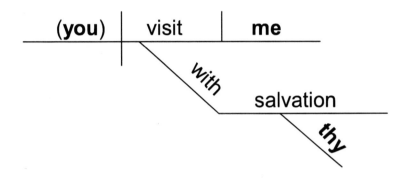

2. **We** have sinned with **our** fathers. (Psalm 106:6a)

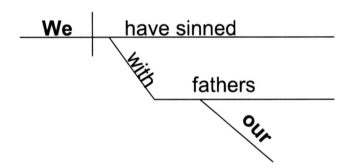

3. **He** [the LORD] led **them** forth by the right way. (Psalm 107:7a)

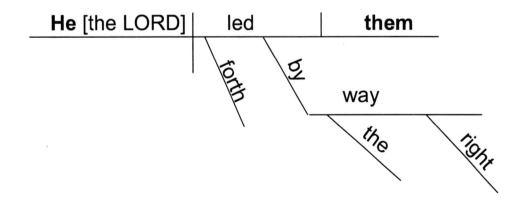

## 21 - **Pronouns** - Test Answers

4. **She** [a virtuous woman] will do **him** good and not evil all the days of **her** life. (Proverbs 31:12)

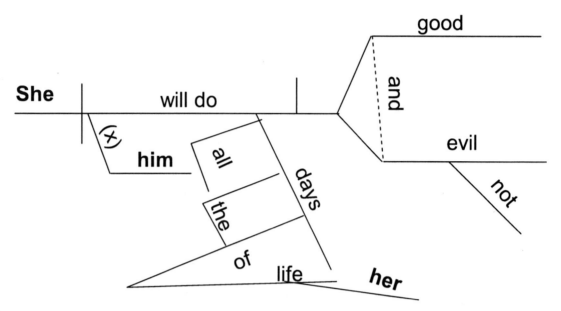

5. The ants are a people not strong, yet **they** prepare **their** meat in the summer. (Proverbs 30:25)

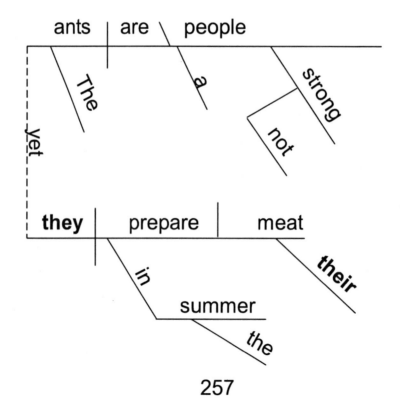

# 22 - Infinitives - Practice Answers

1. The fear of the LORD is to hate evil. (Proverbs 8:13a)

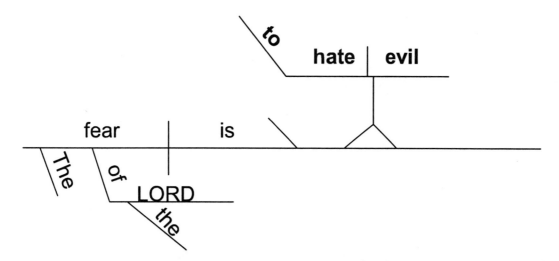

2. He (the Spirit of the LORD) hath sent **me to heal the brokenhearted**. (The subject of the infinitive is always in the objective case. "Me" is the object pronoun form.)

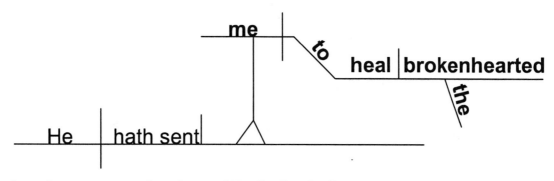

3. Lo, I come to do thy will, O God. (Hebrews 10:9a)

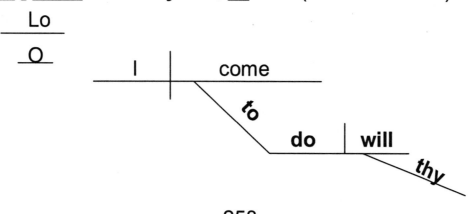

## 22 - **Infinitives** - Practice Answers

4. <u>Let</u> **her own works praise her in the gates**.
   (Proverbs 31:31b)

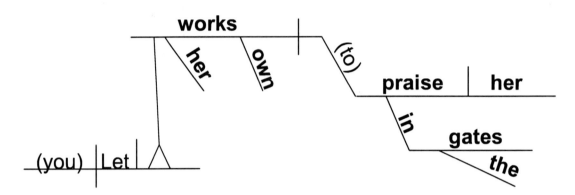

5. The <u>wisdom</u> of the <u>prudent</u> <u>is</u> **to understand his way**.
   (Proverbs 14:8a)

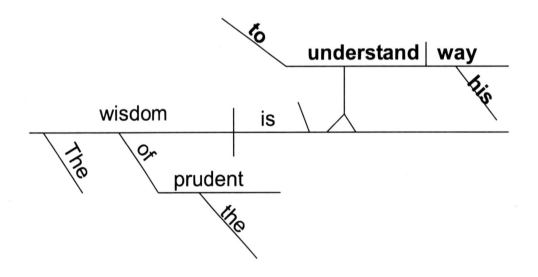

## 22 - **Infinitives** - Test Answers

1. **To do good** <u>and</u> **to communicate** <u>forget</u> <u>not</u>.
   (Hebrews 13:16a)

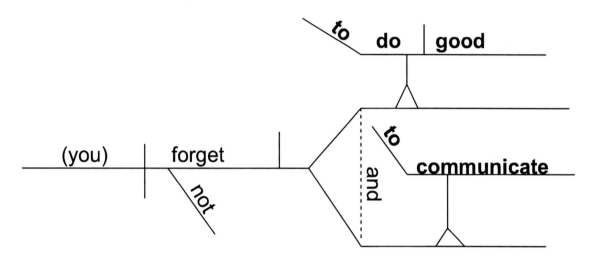

2. <u>The</u> <u>LORD</u> <u>make</u> **you to increase** <u>and</u> **abound in love**.
   (1 Thessalonians 3:12a)

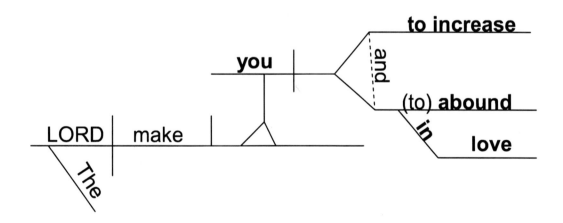

## 22 - Infinitives - Test Answers

3. <u>Let</u> **no man despise thy youth**. (1 Timothy 4:12a)

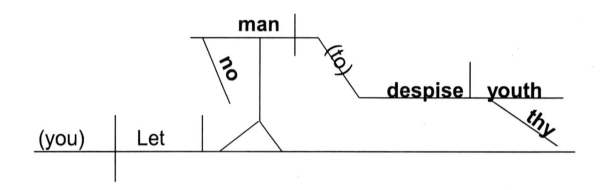

4. <u>Go</u> <u>not</u> <u>forth</u> <u>hastily</u> **to strive**. (Proverbs 25:8a)

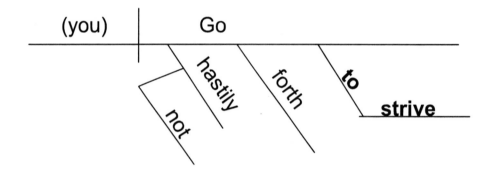

## 22 - **Infinitives** - Test Answers

5. <u>Let</u> **us consider one another to provoke unto love** <u>and</u> **to good works**. (Hebrews 10:24)

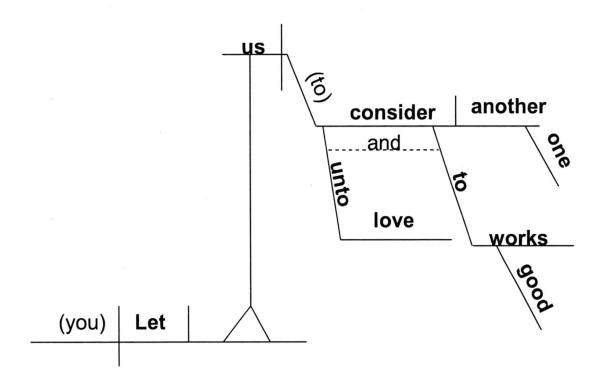

The subject of the infinitive phrase is always in the objective case. "Us" is an objective plural pronoun.

## 23 - **Gerunds** - Practice Answers

1. Remove from me the way of **lying**. (Psalm 119:29a)

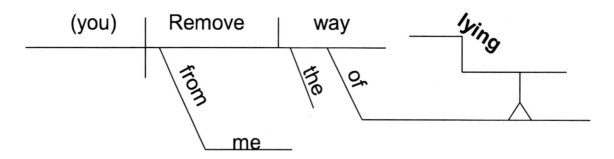

2. Give me **understanding**, and I shall keep thy law. (Psalm 119:34a)

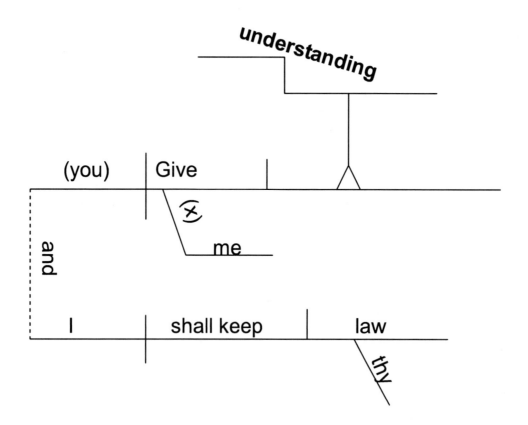

## 23 - **Gerunds** - Practice Answers

3. I hate and abhor **lying**: but thy law do I love. (Psalm 119:163)

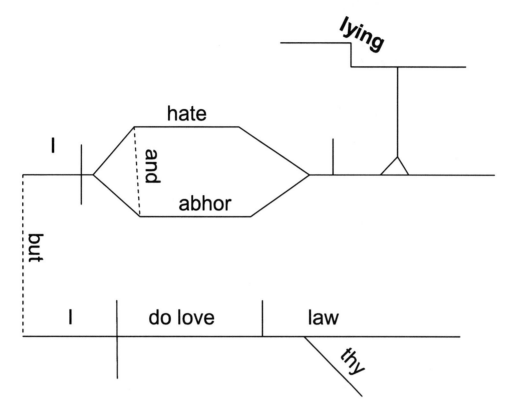

4. **Blessings** are upon the head of the just. (Proverbs 10:6a)

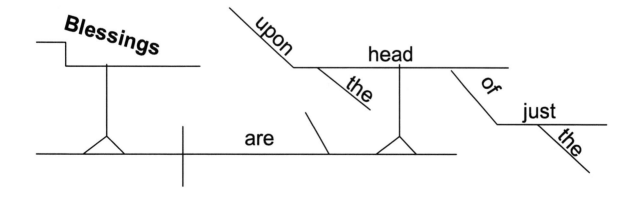

## 23 - **Gerunds** - Practice Answers

5. Good **understanding** giveth favour. (Proverbs 13:15a)

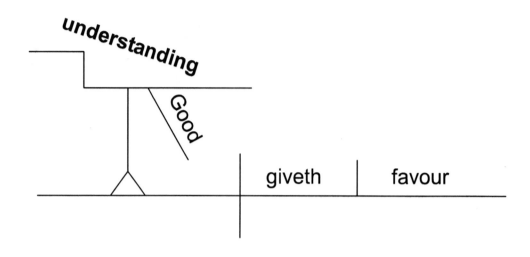

## 23 - **Gerunds** - Test Answers

1. My son, God will provide himself a lamb for a burnt **offering**. (Genesis 22:8a)

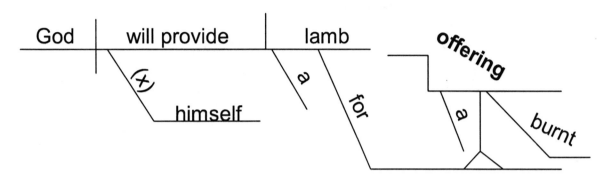

2. Turn away mine eyes from **beholding** vanity. (Psalm 119:37a)

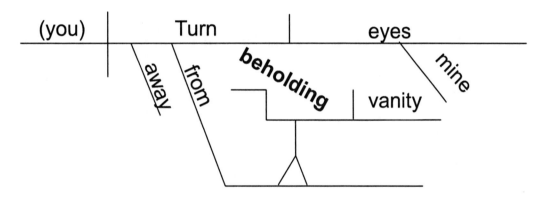

3. Without **shedding** of blood is no remission. (Hebrews 9:22b)

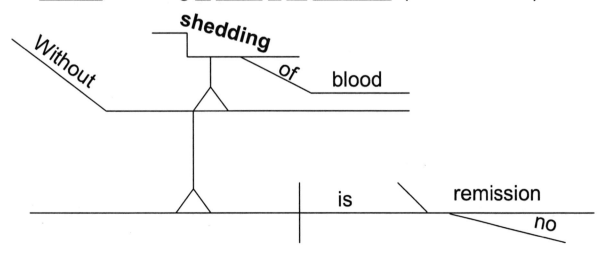

## 23 - **Gerunds** - Test Answers

4. The righteous eateth to the **satisfying** of his soul. (Proverbs 13:25a)

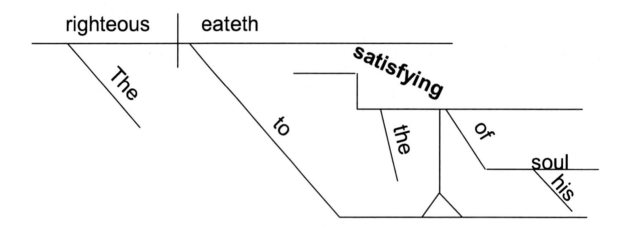

5. Even a child is known by his **doings**. (Proverbs 20:11a)

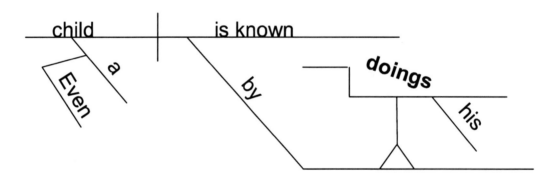

## 24 - **Appositives** - Practice Answers

1. I **Jesus** have sent mine angel to testify unto you these things in the churches. (Revelation 22:16a)

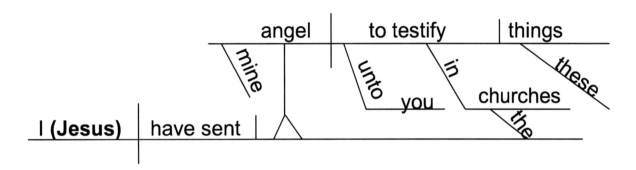

2. I **the LORD** will hear them. (Isaiah 41:17c)

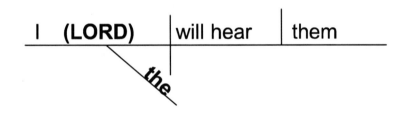

3. Alexander **the coppersmith** did me much evil. (2 Timothy 4:14a)

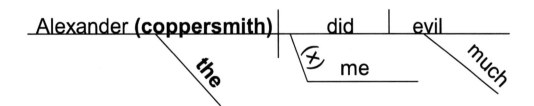

## 24 - **Appositives** - Practice Answers

4. The word of the LORD came expressly unto Ezekiel **the priest**. (Ezekiel 1:3a)

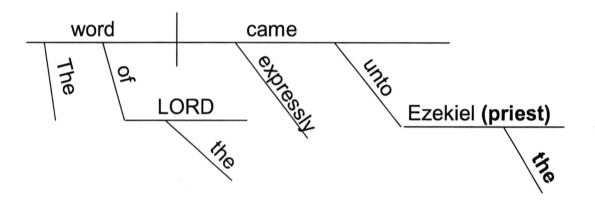

5. Thou art the Christ, **the Son of the living God**. (Matthew 16:16b)

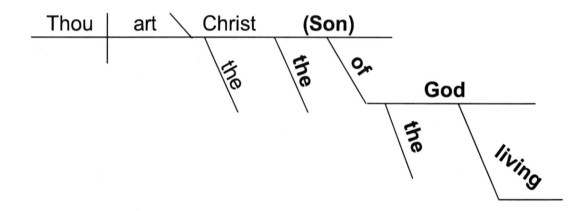

## 24 - **Appositives** - Test Answers

1. God is our refuge and strength, **a very present help in trouble**. (Psalm 46:1)

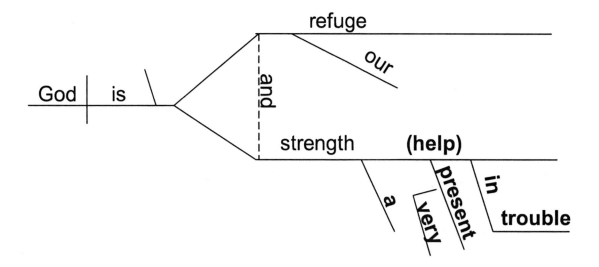

2. The LORD also will be a refuge for the oppressed, **a refuge in times of trouble**. (Psalm 9:9)

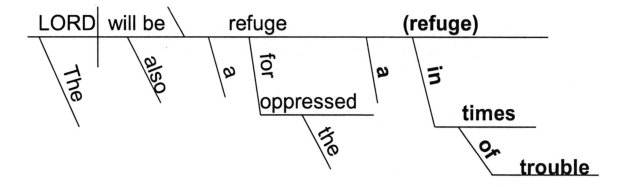

## 24 - **Appositives** - Test Answers

3. The LORD is good, **a strong hold in the day of trouble**. (Nahum 1:7a)

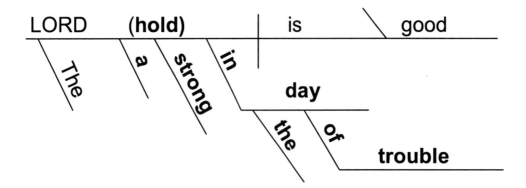

4. Salute Urbane, **our helper in Christ**. (Romans 16:9a)

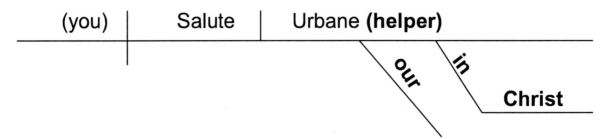

5. Be not thou therefore ashamed of the testimony of our Lord, nor of me **his prisoner**. (2 Timothy 1:8a)

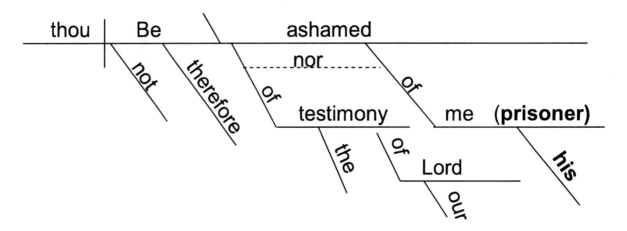

## 25 - **Nouns of Direct Address** - Practice Answers

1. **Little children**, keep yourselves from idols. Amen. (1 John 5:21)

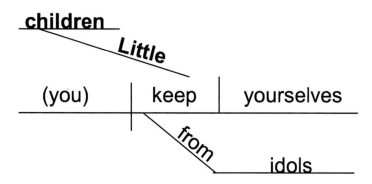

2. Who art thou, **LORD**? (Acts 9:5a)

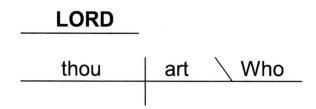

3. Lo, I come to do thy will, O **God**. (Hebrews 10:9a)

    Lo

    O

    **God**

## 25 - **Nouns of Direct Address** - Practice Answers

4. **LORD**, evermore give us this bread. (John 6:34b)

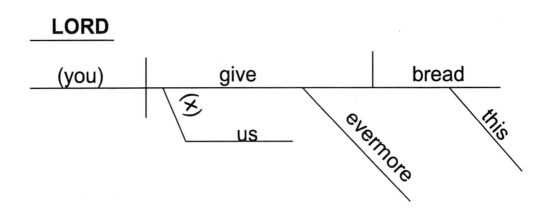

5. **My son**, God will provide himself a lamb for a burnt offering. (Genesis 22:8a)

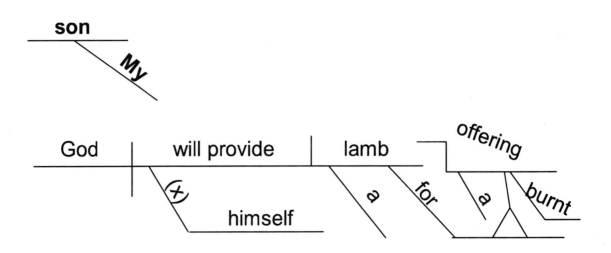

## 25 - **Nouns of Direct Address** - Test Answers

1. <u>Now</u>, **little children**, <u>abide</u> <u>in</u> <u>him</u>. (1 John 2:28a)

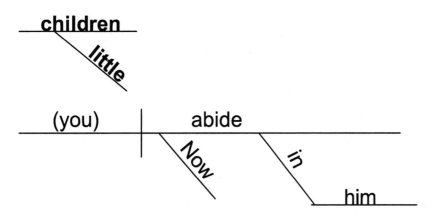

2. <u>Why</u> <u>are</u> <u>ye</u> <u>fearful,</u> <u>O</u> **ye of little faith**? (Matthew 8:26a)

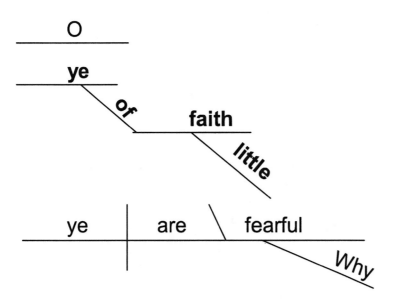

3. **Son of man**, <u>can</u> <u>these</u> <u>bones</u> <u>live</u>? (Ezekiel 37:3a)

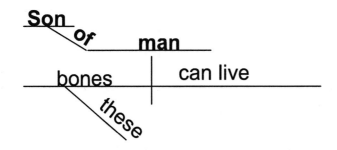

## 25 - **Nouns of Direct Address** -Test Answers

4. **LORD**, teach us to pray. (Luke 11:1c)

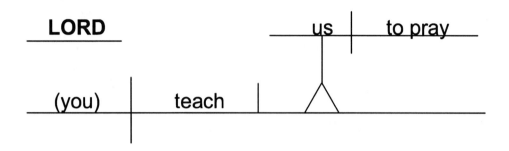

5. Bless the LORD, O my soul. (Psalm 103:1a)

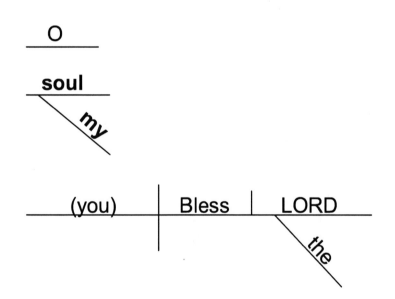

## 26 - Unit 2 - Test Answers

1. I waited patiently for the LORD; and he inclined unto me, and heard my cry. (Psalm 40:1)

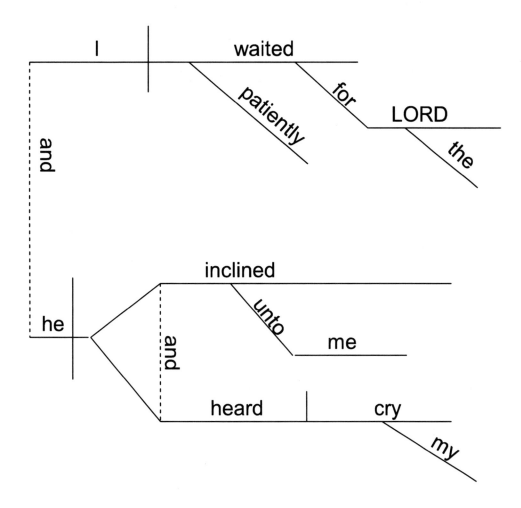

2. The statutes of the LORD are right, rejoicing the heart. (Psalm 19:8a)

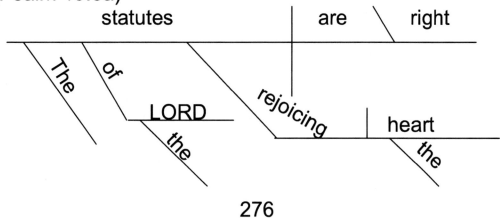

## 26 - Unit 2 - Test Answers

3. Many, O LORD my God, are thy wonderful works *which thou hast done*. (Psalm 40:5a)

*Which thou hast done* has not yet been explained.

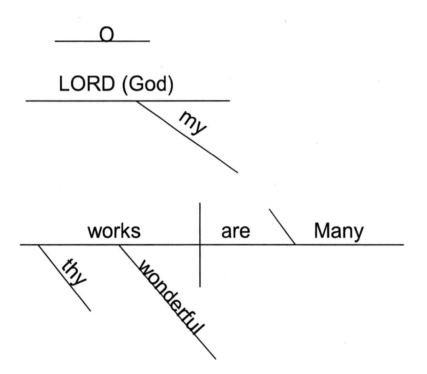

## 26 - Unit 2 - Test Answers

4. Be pleased, O LORD, to deliver me. (Psalm 40:13a)

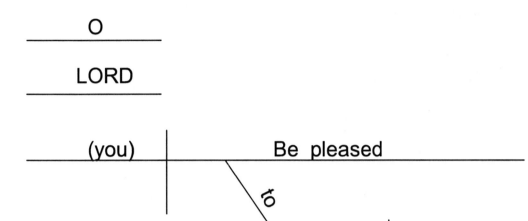

5. The fear of the LORD is the beginning of wisdom. (Psalm 111:10a)

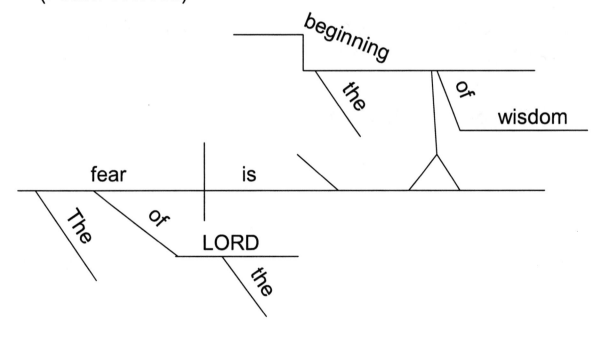

# 27 - Unit 3 - **Noun Clauses** - Practice Answers

1. **Whoso putteth his trust in the LORD** <u>shall</u> <u>be</u> <u>safe</u>. (Proverbs 29:25b)

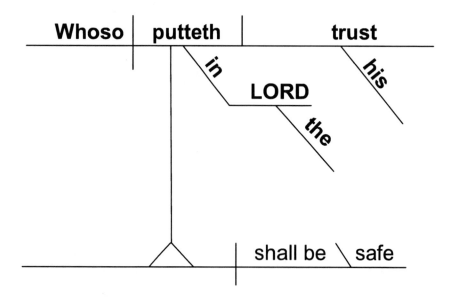

2. **Whosoever shall call upon the name of the LORD** <u>shall</u> <u>be</u> <u>saved</u>. (Romans 10:13)

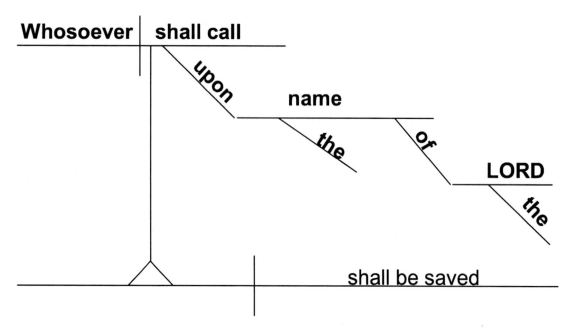

# 27 - Noun Clauses - Practice Answers

3. This is love, that we walk after his commandments. (2 John 1:6a)

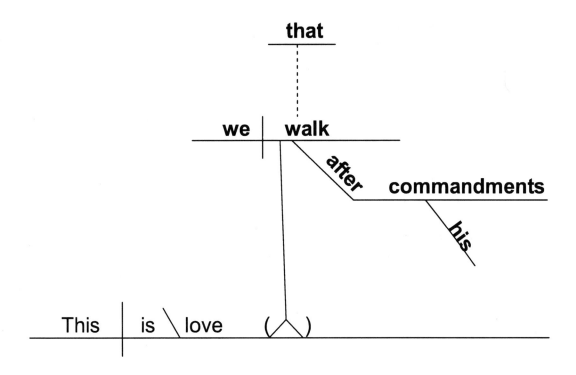

4. Be still, and know that I am God. (Psalm 46:10a)

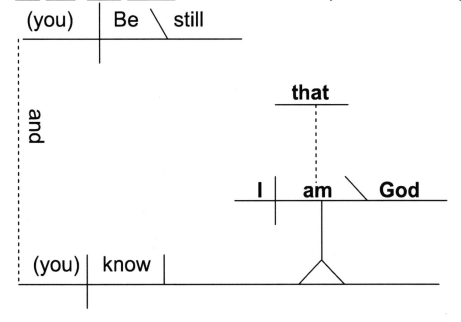

## 27 - **Noun Clauses** - Practice Answers

**5. Whosoever denieth the Son**, the same hath not the Father. (1 John 2:23a)

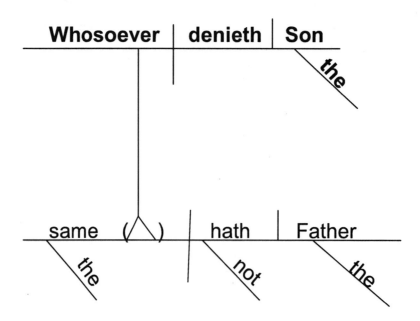

## 27 - **Noun Clauses** - Test Answers

1. <u>See</u> **that ye love one another with a pure heart fervently.** (1 Peter 1:22b)

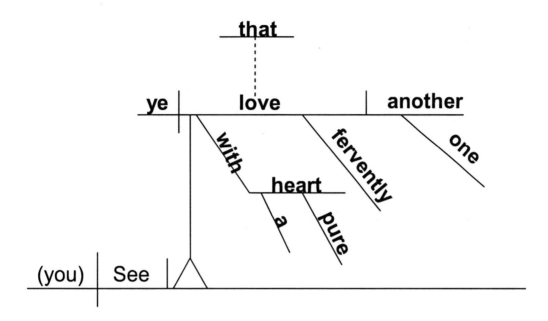

2. It <u>doth</u> <u>not</u> <u>yet</u> <u>appear</u> **what we shall be.** (1 John 3:2b)

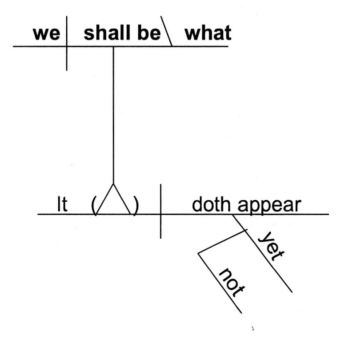

## 27 - **Noun Clauses** - Test Answers

3. **Whosoever believeth that Jesus is the Christ** is born of God. (1 John 5:1a)

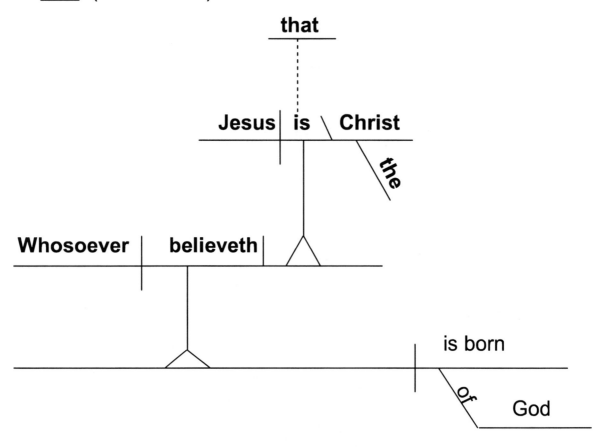

4. I know **that the LORD is great**. (Psalm 135:5a)

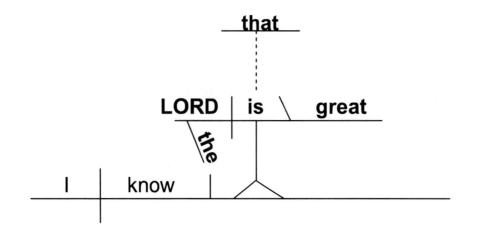

27 - **Noun Clauses** - Test Answers

5. The fire shall try every man's work of **what sort it is**.
   (1 Corinthians 3:13c)

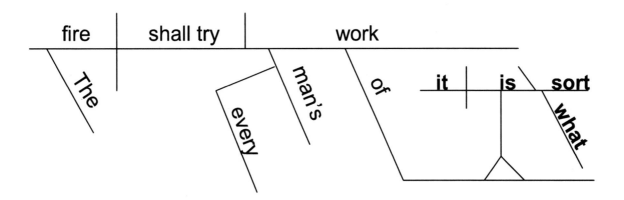

284

## 28 - Adjective Clauses - Practice Answers

1. They that sow in tears shall reap in joy. (Psalm 126:5)

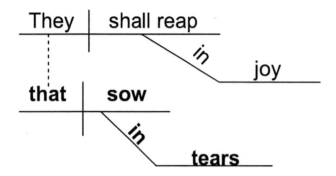

2. Every one that is of the truth heareth my voice. (John 18:37c)

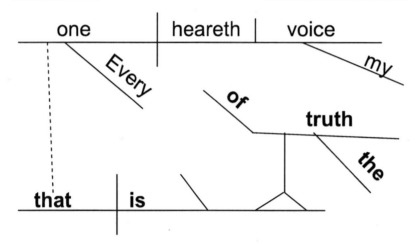

3. The LORD preserveth all them that love him. (Psalm 145:20a)

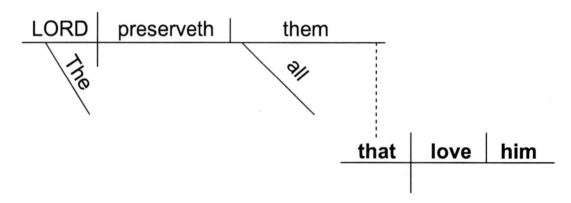

## 28 - **Adjective Clauses** - Practice Answers

4. The grace of God **that bringeth salvation** hath appeared to all men. (Titus 2:11)

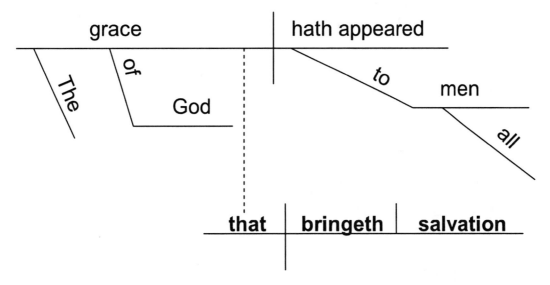

5. Every spirit **that confesseth that Jesus Christ is come in the flesh** is of God. (1 John 4:2b)

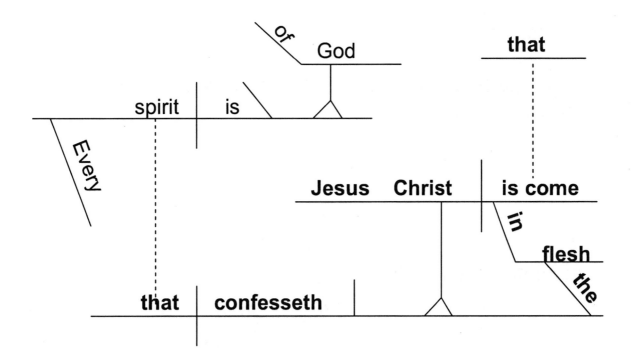

## 28 - Adjective Clauses - Test Answers

1. He **that covereth his sins** shall not prosper.
   (Proverbs 28:13a)

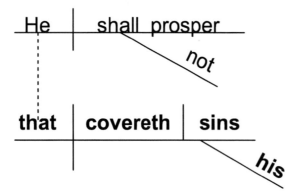

2. A man **that hath friends** must shew himself friendly.
   (Proverbs 18:24a)

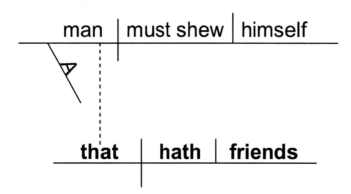

3. He **that hath pity upon the poor** lendeth unto the LORD.
   (Proverbs 19:17a)

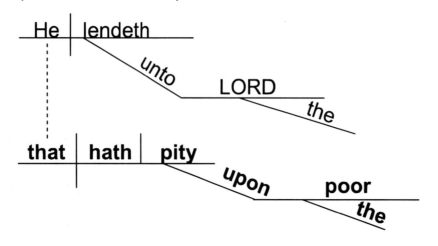

# 28 - **Adjective Clauses** - Test Answers

4. The LORD is known by the judgment **which he executeth**. (Psalm 9:16a)

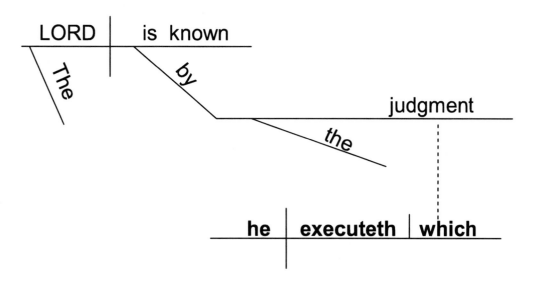

5. They **that deal truly** are his delight. (Proverbs 12:22b)

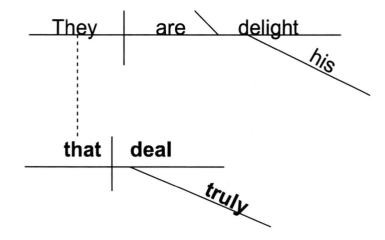

## 29 - **Adverb Clauses** - Practice Answers

1. **When the wicked are multiplied**, transgression increaseth: but the righteous shall see their fall. (Proverbs 29:16)

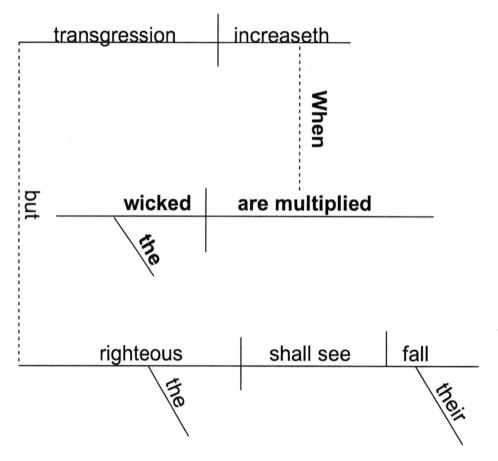

2. **If ye love me**, keep my commandments. (John 14:15)

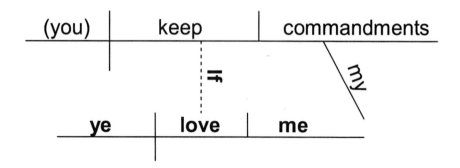

## 29 - **Adverb Clauses** - Practice Answers

3. I will sing unto the LORD, **because he hath dealt bountifully with me**. (Psalm 13:6)

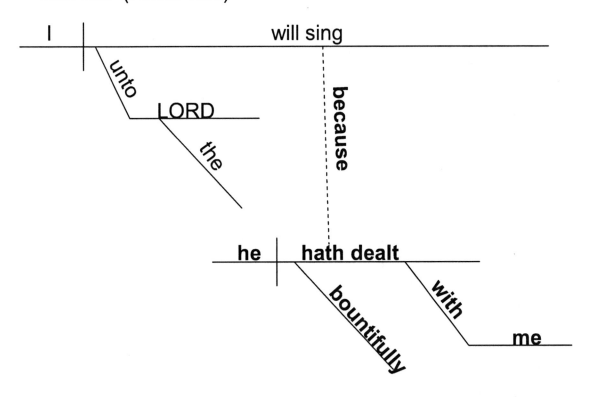

4. The wicked flee **when no man pursueth**. (Proverbs 28:1a)

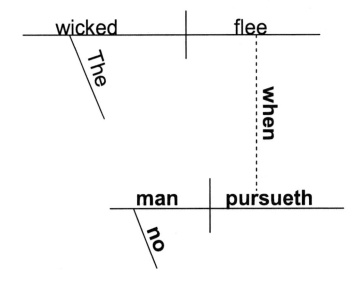

## 29 - **Adverb Clauses** - Practice Answers

5. **Though the LORD be high**, yet hath he respect unto the lowly: but the proud he knoweth afar off.  (Psalm 138:6)

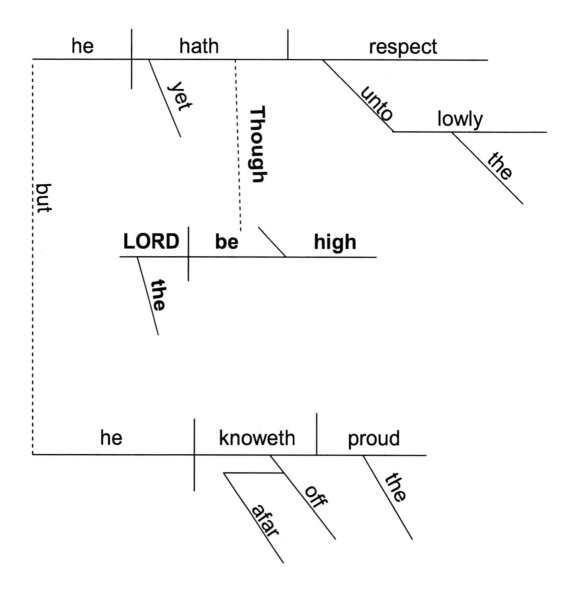

## 29 - **Adverb Clauses** - Test Answers

1. I am the door: **by me if any man enter in**, he shall be saved. (John 10:9a)

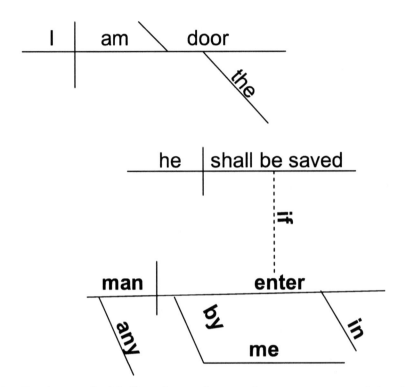

2. Beloved, **if God so loved us**, we ought also to love one another. (1 John 4:11)

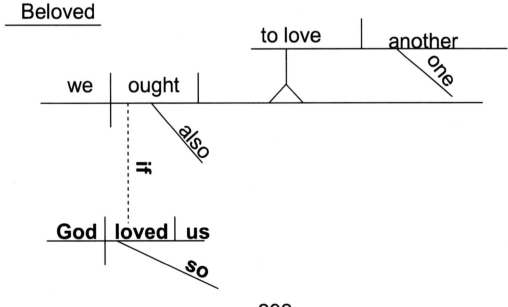

292

## 29 - **Adverb Clauses** - Test Answers

3. **When I became a man**, I put away childish things. (1 Corinthians 13:11b)

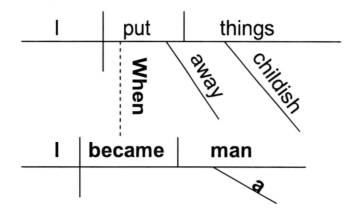

4. **While we were yet sinners**, Christ died for us. (Romans 5:8b)

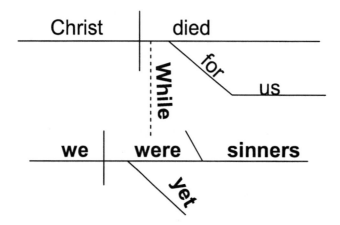

## 29 - **Adverb Clauses** -Test Answers

5. **When the fulness of the time was come,** God sent forth his Son. (Galatians 4:4a)

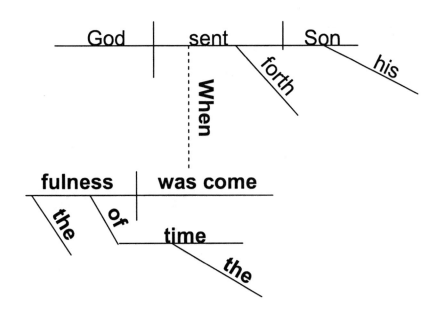

# 30 - Unit 3 - Test Answers

1. I love the LORD, because he hath heard my voice and my supplications. (Psalm 116:1)

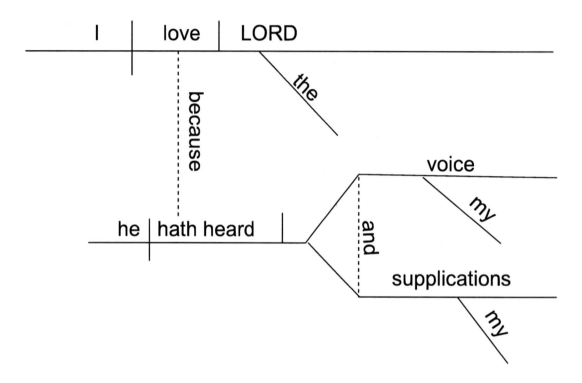

2. This is the day which the LORD hath made. (Psalm 118:24a)

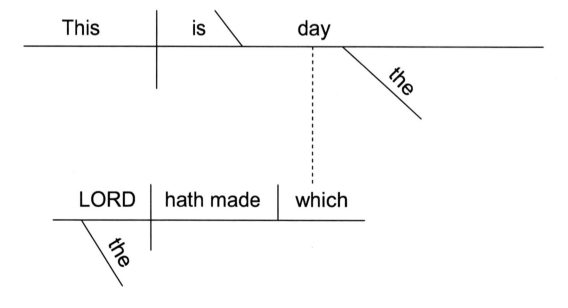

## 30 - Unit 3 - Test Answers

3. I know, O LORD, that thy judgments are right. (Psalm 119:75a)

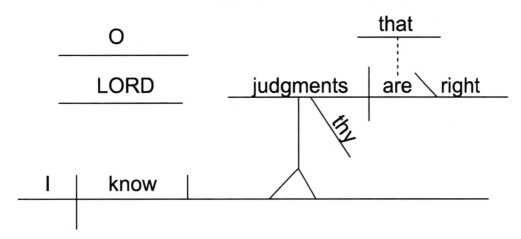

4. Happy is that people, whose God is the LORD. (Psalm 144:15b)

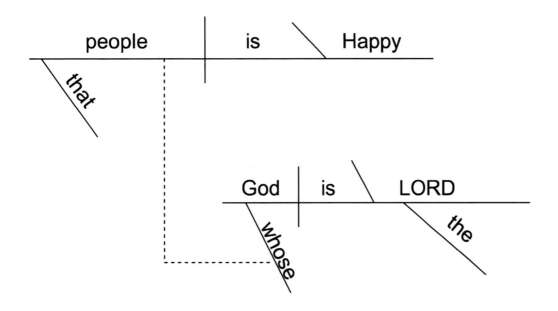

5. Rejoice not when thine enemy falleth. (Proverbs 24:17a)

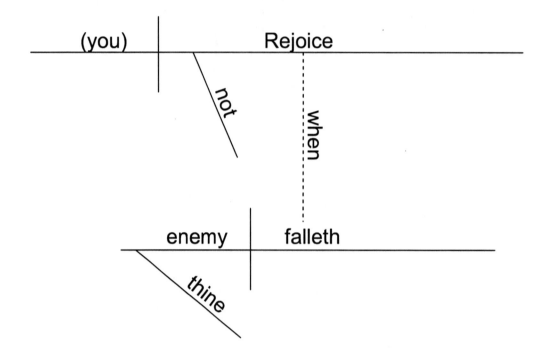

# 31 - Unit 4 - **Simple Sentences** - Practice Answers

1. **The LORD shall judge his people.** (Hebrews 10:30c)

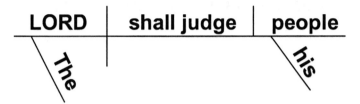

2. **His name is called The Word of God.** (Revelation 19:13b)

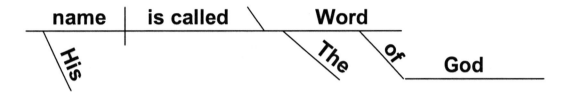

3. **A friend loveth at all times.** (Proverbs 17:17a)

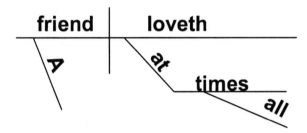

4. **A wise man feareth, and departeth from evil.** (Proverbs 14:16a)

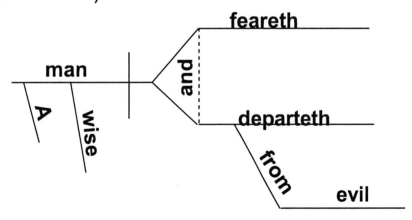

# 31 - **Simple Sentences** - Practice Answers

5. **The Son of man shall come in the glory of his Father with his angels.** (Matthew 16:27a)

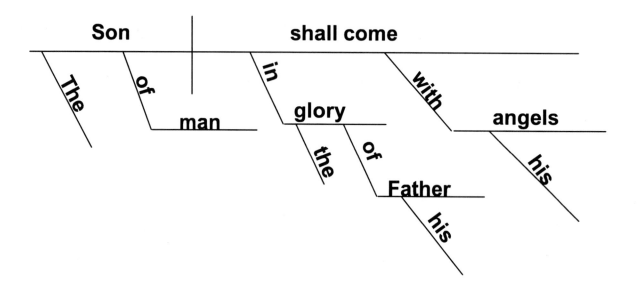

# 31 - **Simple Sentences** - Test Answers

1. **In the beginning God created the heaven and the earth**. (Genesis 1:1)

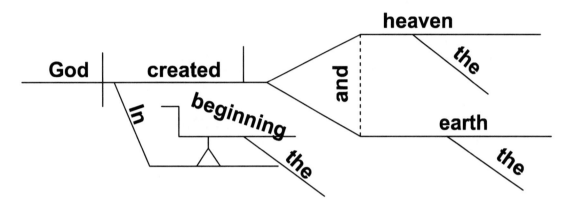

2. **I will confess my transgressions unto the LORD**. (Psalm 32:5b)

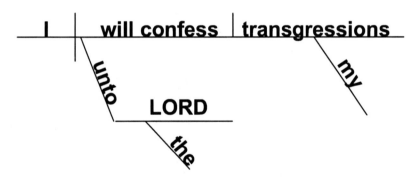

3. **By the works of the law shall no flesh be justified**. (Galatians 2:16c)

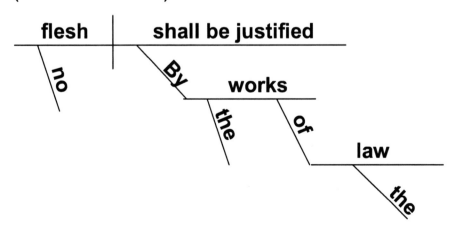

# 31 - **Simple Sentences** -Test Answers

4. **A merry heart doeth good like a medicine.**
   (Proverbs 17:22a)

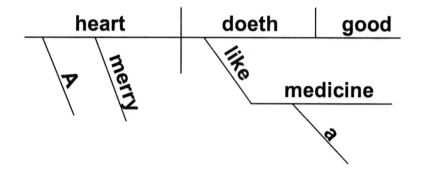

5. **Death and life are in the power of the tongue.**
   (Proverbs 18:21a)

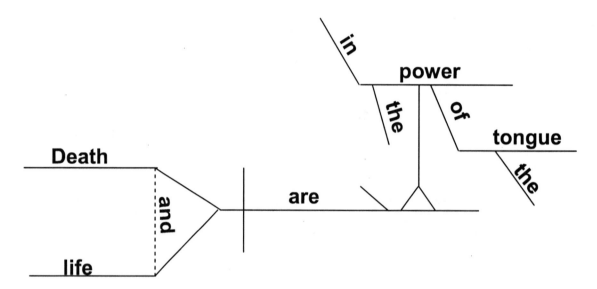

# 32 - Compound Sentences - Practice Answers

1. **Lord, shew us the Father, and it sufficeth us.** (John 14:8)

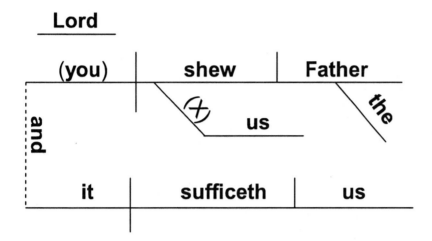

2. **He must increase, but I must decrease.** (John 3:30)

3. **My Father worketh hitherto, and I work.** (John 5:17)

# 32 - **Compound Sentences** - Practice Answers

4. **Judge not according to the appearance, but judge righteous judgment.** (John 7:24)

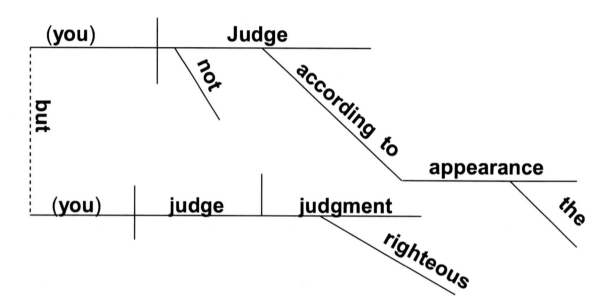

5. **I am crucified with Christ: nevertheless I live**; yet not I, but Christ liveth in me: and the life which I now live in the flesh I live by the faith of the Son of God, who loved me, and gave himself for me. (Galatians 2:20)

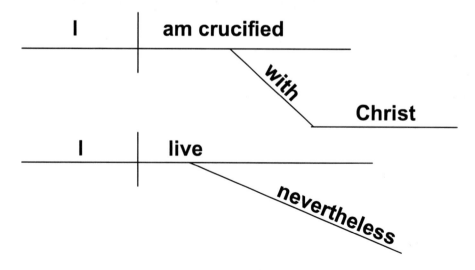

## 32 - **Compound Sentences** - Test Answers

1. **I believed, and therefore have I spoken.**
   (2 Corinthians 4:13b)

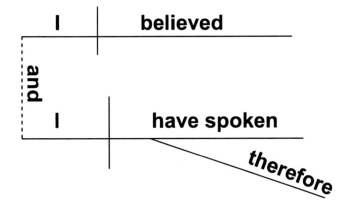

2. **Seek the LORD, and his strength: seek his face evermore.**
   (Psalm 105:4)

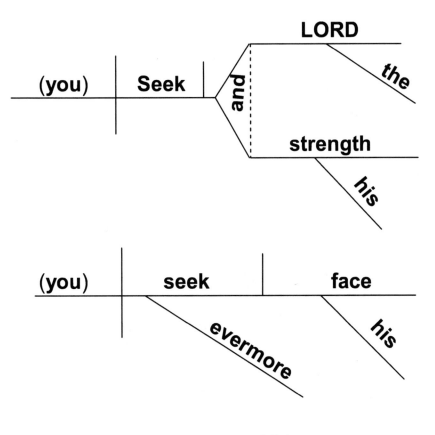

## 32 - Compound Sentences - Test Answers

3. **I have fought a good fight, I have finished my course, I have kept the faith.** (2 Timothy 4:7)

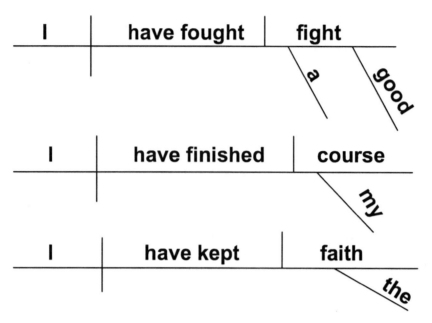

4. **I was a stranger, and ye took me in.** (Matthew 25:35c)

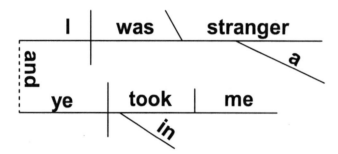

5. **Awake to righteousness, and sin not.**
(1 Corinthians 15:34a)

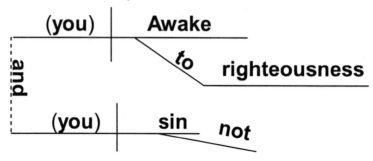

# 33 - **Complex Sentences** - Practice Answers

1. **If any man thirst,** let him come unto me, and drink. (John 7:37b)

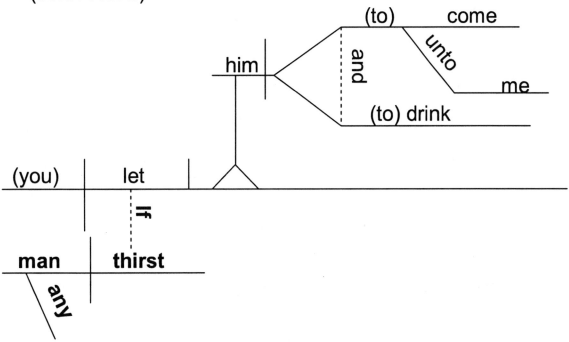

2. The grace of God **that bringeth salvation** hath appeared to all men. (Titus 2:11)

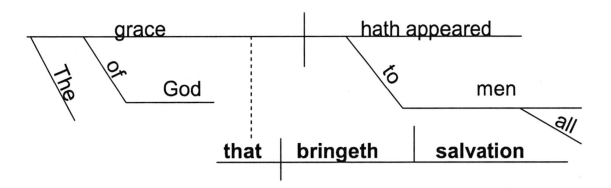

## 33 - **Complex Sentences** - Practice Answers

3. Provide me now a man **that can play well**. (1 Samuel 16:17a)

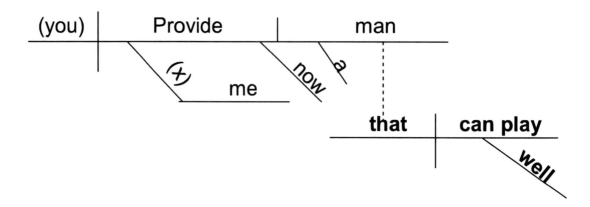

4. He **that trusteth in his riches** shall fall. (Proverbs 11:28a)

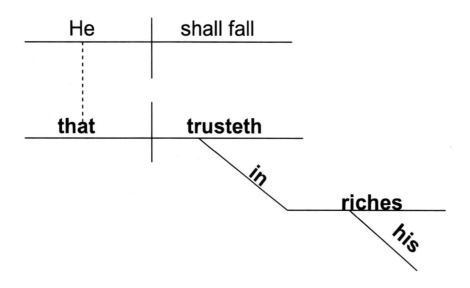

# 33 - **Complex Sentences** - Practice Answers

5. <u>Every</u> <u>one</u> **that is proud in heart** <u>is</u> <u>an</u> <u>abomination</u> <u>to</u> <u>the</u> <u>LORD</u>. (Proverbs 16:5a)

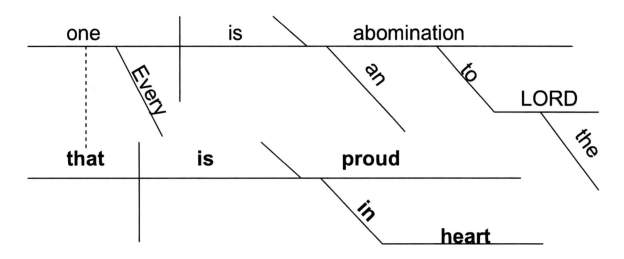

# 33 - Complex Sentences - Test Answers

1. He that hearkeneth unto counsel is wise.
   (Proverbs 12:15b)

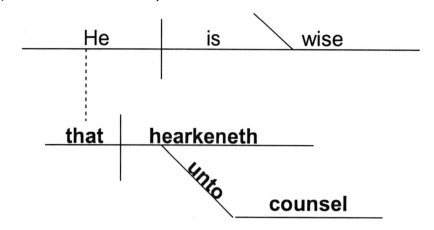

2. A man that hath friends must shew himself friendly.
   (Proverbs 18:24a)

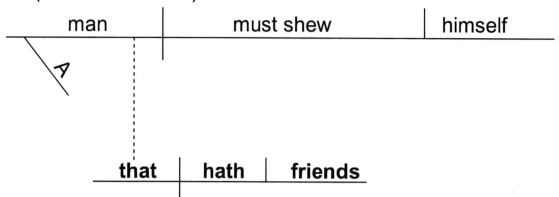

3. The wicked flee when no man pursueth. (Proverbs 28:1a)

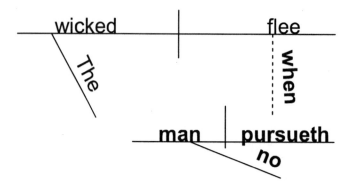

## 33 - **Complex Sentences** - Test Answers

4. **If a house be divided against itself,** that house cannot stand. (Mark 3:25)

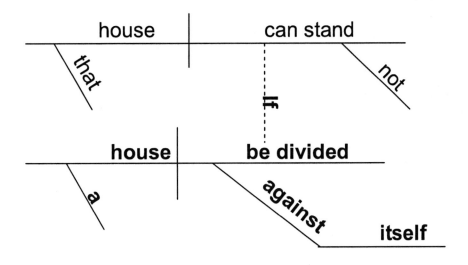

5. I know **that my redeemer liveth**. (Job 19:25a)

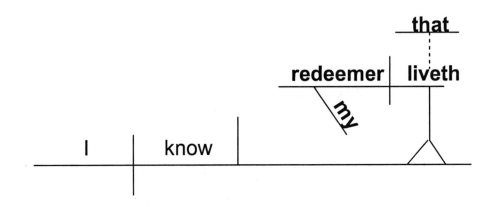

## 34 - Unit 4 - Test Answers

1. Gracious is the LORD, and righteous; yea, our God is merciful. (Psalm 116:5)

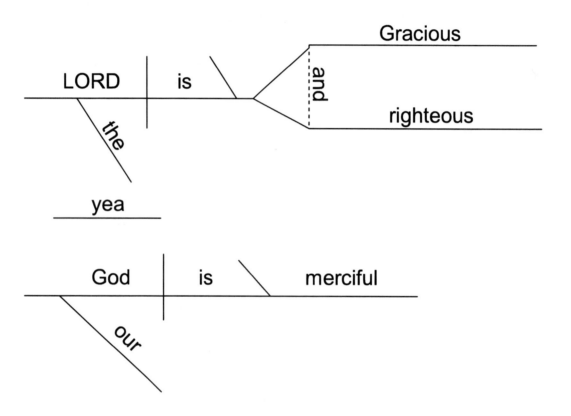

2. To depart from evil is understanding. (Job 28:28b)

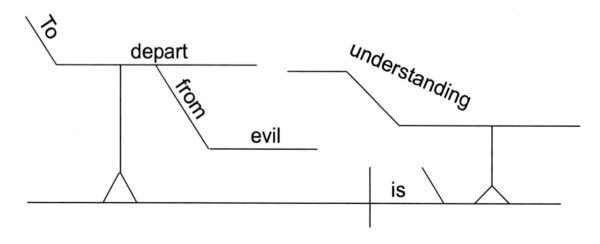

## 34 - Unit 4 - Test Answers

3. Behold, the fear of the Lord, that is wisdom. (Job 28:28a)

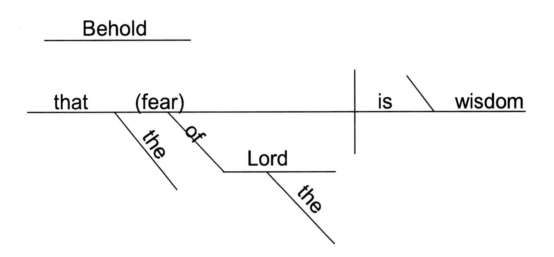

4. I, even I, am the LORD; and beside me there is no saviour. (Isaiah 43:11)

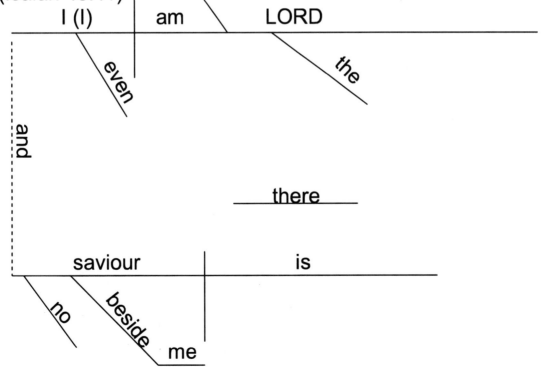

## 34 - Unit 4 - Test Answers

5. If any man be in Christ, he is a new creature. (2 Corinthians 5:17a)

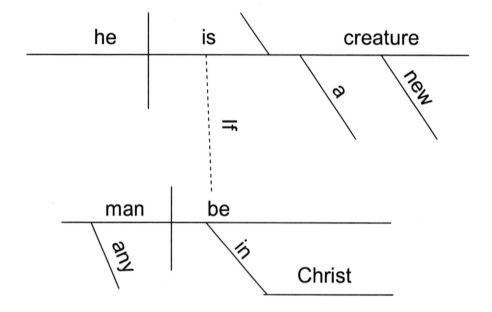

# 35 - Unit 5 - All Units - Test Answers

1. The entrance of thy words giveth light; it giveth understanding unto the simple. (Psalm 119:130)

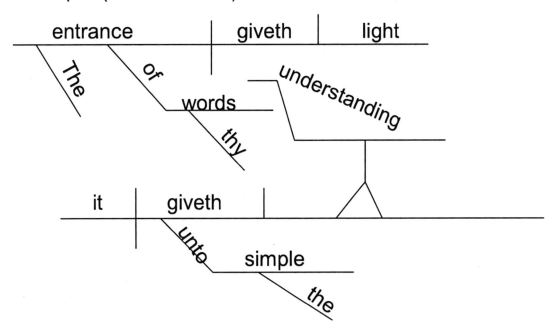

2. He that is of a merry heart hath a continual feast. (Proverbs 15:15b)

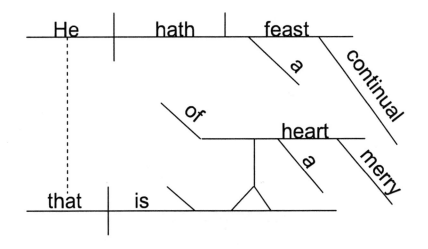

## 35 - All Units - Test Answers

3. Great and marvellous are thy works, Lord God Almighty. (Revelation 15:3b)

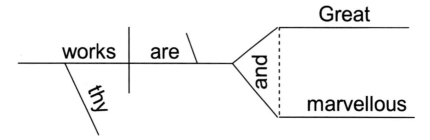

4. My brethren, count it all joy when ye fall into divers temptations. (James 1:2) *All joy* - objective complement.

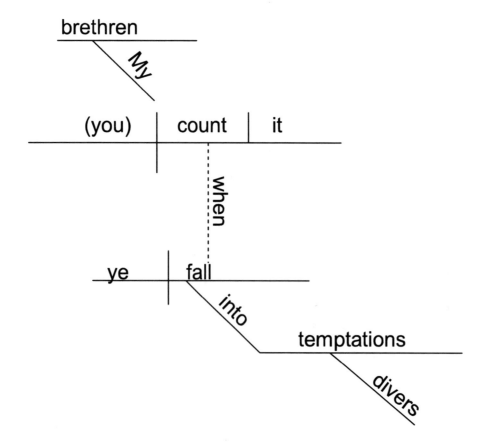

# 35 - All Units - Test Answers

5. My grace is sufficient for thee: for my strength is made perfect in weakness. (2 Corinthians 12:9a)

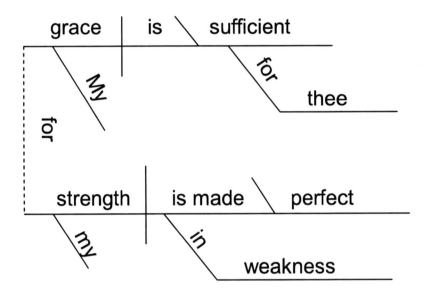

6. A virtuous woman is a crown to her husband. (Proverbs 12:4a)

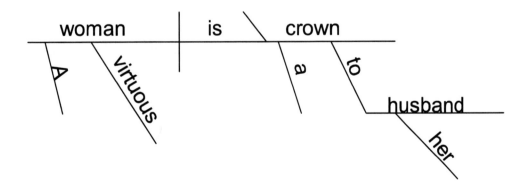

## 35 - All Units - Test Answers

7. Ye do err, not knowing the scriptures, nor the power of God. (Matthew 22:29b)

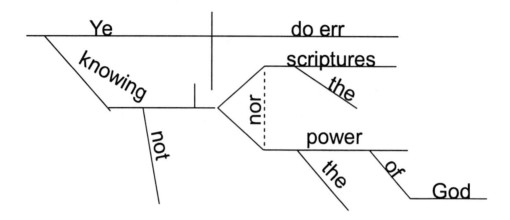

8. Be ye therefore ready also: for the Son of man cometh at an hour when ye think not. (Luke 12:40)

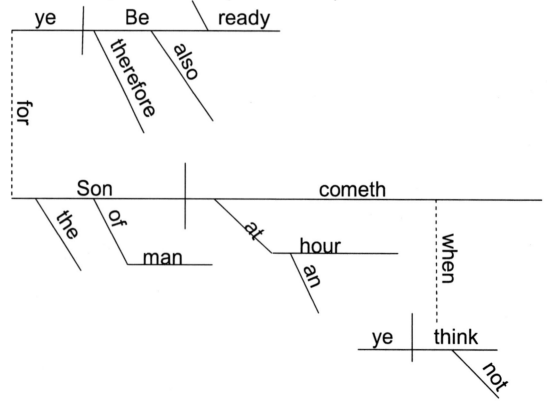

## 35 - All Units - Test Answers

9. The words of a wise man's mouth are gracious. (Ecclesiastes 10:12a)

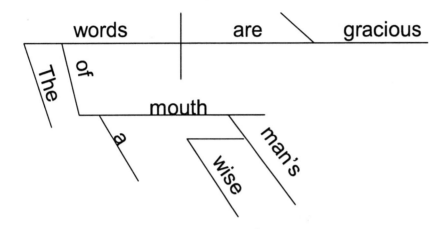

10. A soft answer turneth away wrath. (Proverbs 15:1a)

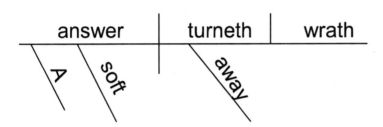

11. Rejoice not when thine enemy falleth. (Proverbs 24:17a)

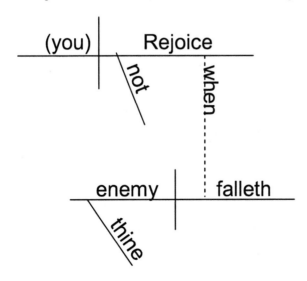

## 35 - All Units - Test Answers

12. Heaven and earth shall pass away, but my words shall not pass away. (Matthew 24:35)

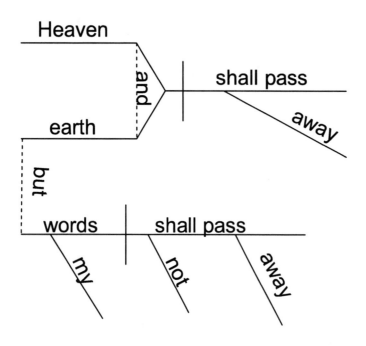

13. A man that hath friends must shew himself friendly. (Proverbs 18:24a)

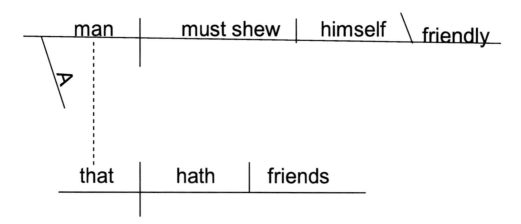

## 35 - All Units - Test Answers

14. God so loved the world, that he gave his only begotten Son, that whosoever believeth in him should not perish, but have everlasting life. (John 3:16)

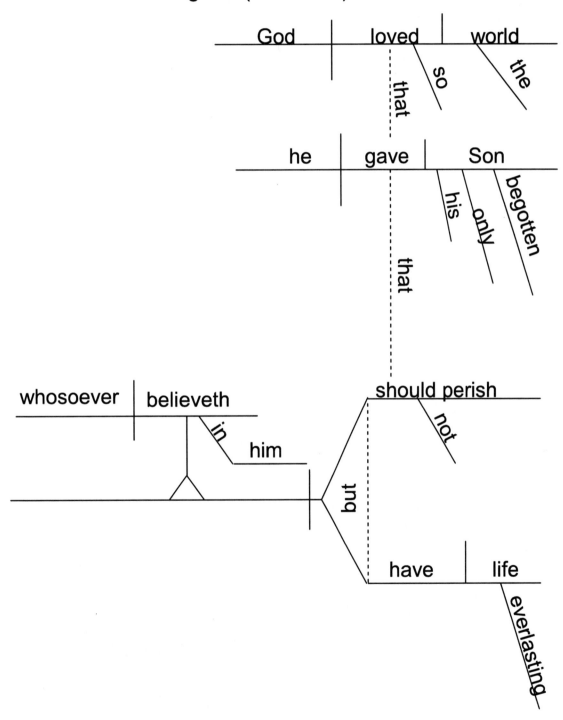

## 35 - All Units - Test Answers

15. Choose you this day whom ye will serve. (Joshua 24:15b)

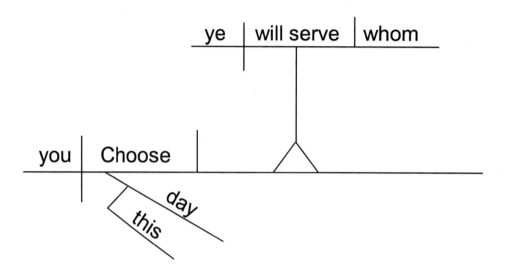

16. I, even I, am he that comforteth you. (Isaiah 51:12a)

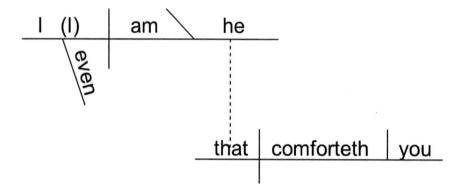

17. Honour thy father and thy mother. (Exodus 20:12a)

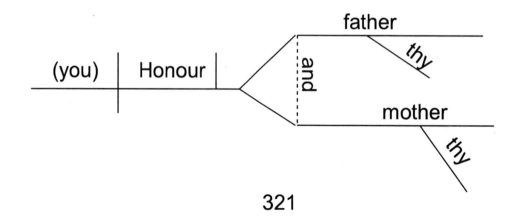

## 35 - All Units - Test Answers

18. With what judgment ye judge, ye shall be judged: and with what measure ye mete, it shall be measured to you again.
    (Matthew 7:2)

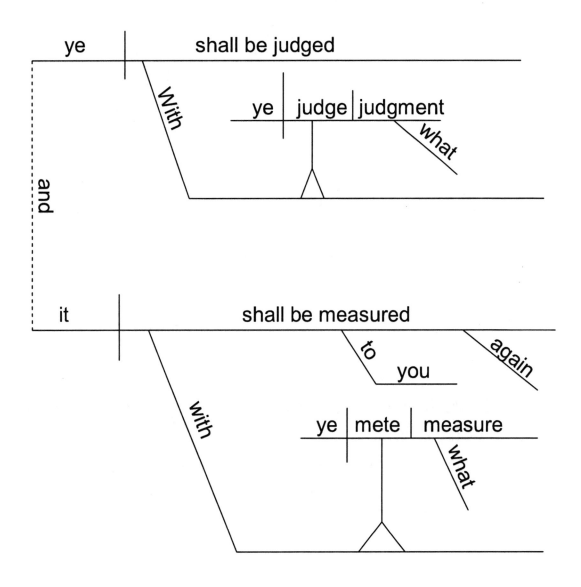

# 35 - All Units - Test Answers

19. I have manifested thy name unto the men which thou gavest me out of the world. (John 17:6a)

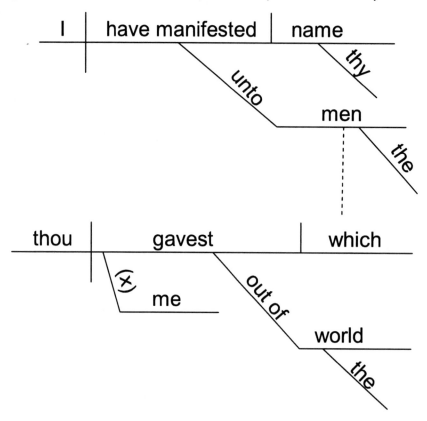

20. I have finished the work which thou gavest me to do. (John 17:4b)

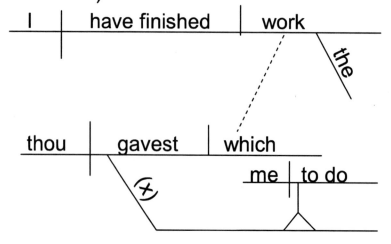

## About the Author

Shirley Forsen became a Christian when she was ten years old. She was graduated from Southwest Baptist University in Bolivar, Missouri and from William Jewell College in Liberty, Missouri. In 1956 she earned a Masters of Religious Education degree from Southern Seminary in Louisville, Kentucky. At Southwest Baptist University she served as Director of Student Religious Activities from 1956 to 1959. She taught English at Butler High School in Butler, Missouri for two years and at the Grandview Junior High School in Grandview, Missouri for twenty-eight years. She now resides at Foxwood Springs Living Center in Raymore, Missouri.

# Glossary

**Adjective** - word that modifies (describes or limits) nouns or pronouns

**Adjective Clause** - a dependent clause used as an adjective to modify (describe or limit) a noun or pronoun

**Adverb** - word that modifies (describes or limits) verbs, adjectives or other adverbs

**Adverb Clause** - a dependent clause which is used as an adverb to modify a verb, verb phrase, verbal, adjective, or adverb

**Appositive** - a noun or noun clause added to another noun or pronoun to further identify it or explain it

**Auxiliary verb** - also called a helping verb, used to "help" another verb in forming voices and tenses

**Clause** - a group of words including a subject and predicate and forming a part of a sentence

**Complement** - a word or expression used to complete the action or idea indicated by a verb

**Complex Sentence** - a sentence consisting of one independent clause and one or more dependent clauses

**Compound Sentence** - a sentence consisting of two or more independent clauses

**Compound-Complex Sentence** - a sentence consisting of two or more independent clauses and one or more dependent clauses

**Conjunction** - a word used to connect words or groups of words such as phrases and clauses

**Conjunctive adverb** - an adverb used as a conjunction to connect a dependent clause to an independent clause

**Coordinating conjunction** - a conjunction linking words, phrases, or clauses of equal rank

**Correlative conjunction** - coordinating conjunctions used in pairs to connect words of equal grammatical value

**Direct object** - a noun or a pronoun that receives the action of the verb

**Gerund** - a verb used as a noun

**Indefinite pronoun** - a pronoun that refers to no specific person, place or thing

**Independent clause** - a clause that expresses a complete thought

**Indirect object** - a noun or a pronoun that precedes a direct object of a verb and tells to whom or for whom something is done

**Infinitive** - the word "to" plus a verb

**Intensive pronoun** - a pronoun ending with *-self*

**Interjection** - an exclamatory word expressing strong feeling or surprise

**Interrogative pronoun** - a pronoun used in a question: *who, which, what, whoever, whatever, where, when, why, how*

**Linking verb -** a non-action verb that expresses a state of being or fixed condition. It "links" a subject to a noun, pronoun, or adjective in the predicate.

**Modify** - to describe or limit

**Nominals** - words that function as nouns but aren't nouns themselves

**Noun** - a part of speech that names a person, place, thing, idea

**Object of a preposition** - a noun or pronoun following a preposition

**Participle** - a verb form functioning as an adjective

**Part of speech** - a classification for every word in a language in English; the primary parts of speech are as follows: *noun, pronoun, verb, adverb, adjective, preposition, conjunction,* and *interjection*

**Personal pronoun** - a pronoun referring to a person

**Phrase** - a group of related words not containing a subject and predicate

**Plural** - more than one

**Predicate** - the verb or verb phrase that makes a statement about the subject

**Predicate adjective** - an adjective placed in a predicate after a linking verb and used to modify the subject of a sentence or a clause

**Preposition** - a part of speech before a noun or pronoun showing the relationship of that noun or pronoun (object) to some other word in the sentence

**Prepositional phrase** - a preposition plus its object and related words

**Pronoun** - a word that takes the place of a noun

**Reflexive pronoun** - a pronoun ending in *-self* and referring to the subject

**Relative pronoun** - a pronoun connecting or relating an adjective clause to an antecedent

**Simple sentence** - a sentence containing one subject and one predicate

**Simple subject** - noun or pronoun without any modifiers acting as a subject

**Simple predicate** - verb without any modifiers or objects acting as the main verb of a clause

**Singular** - one

**Subject** - the doer of the action of the verb

**Subordinating conjunction** - a conjunction connecting a dependent clause to an independent clause

**Tense** - the time of the action or state of being expressed in a verb

**Verb** - a part of speech expressing *action* or *state of being*, or *helping* another verb

**Verb phrase** - a group of words consisting of a verb and its helpers

**Verbal** - a verb form used as another part of speech: *gerunds, participles,* and *infinitives*

CPSIA information can be obtained at www.ICGtesting.com
Printed in the USA
LVOW091656100912
298212LV00004B/53/P